Cooking the Catch

Cooking the Catch

Fresh New Zealand Seafood Recipes

Ray McVinnie

REED

For J. and dinners at home.

Published by Reed Books, a division of Reed Publishing (NZ) Ltd, 39 Rawene Rd, Birkenhead, Auckland. Associated companies, branches and representatives throughout the world.

ISBN 0 7900 0594 8

© 1986 Ray McVinnie

First published as the *New Zealand Fish Cookbook* by Reed Methuen 1986
New edition 1997

The author asserts his moral rights in the work.

Cover designed by Michele Stutton
Text designed by Clair Stutton

Printed in New Zealand by Wright and Carman (NZ) Limited, Wellington

Contents

Introduction

This is a personal collection of fish and seafood recipes gathered over the years from articles published in *Cuisine* magazine, classes taught at the Epicurean Workshop, menus served in the restaurants in which I have worked and meals cooked at home. Whether you have caught the fish yourself, or it has been bought from that valuable resource, the local fish shop, I hope these recipes will expand the repertoire of the home cook.

In New Zealand we are blessed with an abundance of fresh fish and seafood which is easily accessible. Combined with our excellent produce, New Zealand has the resources for a superb and distinct seafood cuisine. The attitude and circumstances which have over a long period of time created the world's great cuisines are not things which involve the whims of fashion or a pedantic regard for cooking. Care about the food one eats, getting the maximum flavour and goodness and thus enjoyment and value from food, and an attitude which sees eating as important to the everyday social fabric of one's life are far more important to this process.

It is well to remember that restaurant food belongs to the professional chef. Do not waste your time trying to imitate professionals doing a specialised job. If you want to eat that sort of food, go to a restaurant. The difference in appearance between good domestic and restaurant cookery is only a question of style and technique. If intimidated by the fanciful presentations of some chefs, be comforted that most great cuisines are based on well-developed domestic cookery .

Do not mistake simple food for plain food. Fried fish, green salad and crusty bread will be sensational if the fish is fresh and carefully fried in good olive oil and the bread and salad are chosen and prepared with the same care. If they are not, they are boring. Expertly cooked imaginative simple dishes generally impress people more than complicated cookery. The sigh of satisfaction at the end of a well-cooked simple meal from happy diners will probably exceed that at the end of a rich and fussy meal. This is particularly true when cooking fish and seafood. Fish is a delicate commodity; the flavour is easily destroyed by overprocessing and overcooking.

I wanted this book to be useful to people who like cooking and who want to be able to use what is available so I have not concentrated on recipes for rare fish species seldom encountered. The recipes begin with fresh ingredients, often using vegetables and herbs to not only complement the fish and seafood but to add body and savour. This eliminates the need for time-consuming stocks and sauces or the insidious 'preprepared product' which is rarely necessary in the kitchen of the interested cook who likes to retain control over his or her diet and the taste of the food being cooked.

In this collection of recipes, I have borrowed freely from my knowledge of other cuisines in trying to show the versatility of New Zealand fish and seafood. I have experimented as much as possible with fish varieties and tastes to go with them and I encourage the interested cook to do the same, especially since more than one type of fish is suitable for each recipe. It is up to you to decide what is to your taste and how to use what is available. As you proceed I am sure your family and friends will be agreeably surprised and delighted by your competence and originality.

Ray McVinnie

Choosing and cleaning fish

The best fish is that which you have caught yourself; however, this is not always possible, so when buying fish remember that freshness is paramount. Frozen fish is a waste of time and money.

When choosing a whole fish look for the following characteristics. The eyes must be bright. In fish that is not fresh the eyes are opaque and sunken. The skin under the gills should be red, not grey. The skin should glisten and there should be no grit or blobs of slime. Push the flesh with your finger. If it stays dented, do not buy it. If you really doubt its freshness check the smell. Fresh fish smells like fresh sea water.

If the fish is filleted the flesh should look plump and juicy. It should be white with rosy tints. A puddle of cloudy liquid in the tray in which it is displayed is a telltale sign that the fish is not fresh. It should smell, of course, like clean sea water.

Shellfish must come from unpolluted water. This is not a problem when buying from a reputable fishmonger as bad shellfish is bad for business, but you do need to be careful when gathering shellfish yourself. Never use shellfish that have opened and will not close after a second tap on the shell. Like fish, shellfish must smell fresh.

Cleaning whole fish

Cut off any sharp fins. Hold the fish by the tail and, using a blunt knife, scrape the scales towards the head. You will be surprised how easy it is to remove them.

Once all the scales have been removed, slit the belly the length of the fish and remove the guts. Do not throw away any roes as these are good to eat.

Wash the fish under running water to remove any blood, and pat it dry with paper towels.

Fish

stock

1 kg white fish trimmings or carcasses
1 onion, 1 small carrot, 1 stick of celery —
all thinly chopped
thyme, parsley and a bay leaf tied together into
a bouquet garni
1/2 litre white wine
cold water

While liquid fish stock is available commercially it is well to know how to make your own if you have trimmings and carcasses left over from filleting.

Rinse the fish trimmings or carcasses well, removing all traces of blood and viscera as this can make the stock bitter.

Put them into a heavy saucepan together with the vegetables and herbs. Cover the pan and let the contents sweat on a low heat for 10 minutes. Stir frequently to prevent sticking. (This initial sweating gives a better flavour. If the liquid is added immediately, the juices in the fish and the vegetables will not be released as easily.)

Add the wine, then sufficient cold water to cover the vegetables and fish trimmings. Bring to the boil and skim any residue that rises to the top. Reduce the heat and simmer for 20 minutes. Strain through a very fine sieve.

When cool, refrigerate for up to 2 days or freeze no longer than 1 month, although freezing results in a considerable loss of flavour.

FISH STOCK

Sauces
and
accompaniments

Mayonnaise and variations

Homemade mayonnaise, made with olive oil and served with carefully poached white fish or steamed seafood, or plainly grilled, barbecued or panfried fish and seafood always pleases. It has nothing to do with the commercial mixtures that go by the same name and it is easy to make. All you have to remember is to have all equipment and ingredients at room temperature, and do not hurry. A food processor helps.

> **3 egg yolks**
> **1 tsp lemon juice or wine vinegar (do not use**
> **malt vinegar as the flavour is too harsh)**
> **300 ml olive oil**
> **salt**

Beat the egg yolks with the lemon juice or wine vinegar.

When the yolks have thickened a little, start adding the olive oil, drop by drop to make an emulsion. If you add the oil too fast it will curdle.

After about a third of the oil has been 'dropped' in, the dressing should start to look thick and fluffy.

Then, and only then, increase the oil to a trickle and continue until it has all been used. The mayonnaise should look thick and buttery. Taste it and season it as you would a boiled egg. It will need salt and possibly more lemon or vinegar, but do not mistake the need for salt for a deficiency of vinegar. This is a common mistake.

If you do curdle the mayonnaise do not panic. Just take a clean bowl, another egg yolk, beat it and, drop by drop, add the curdled mixture to it. Do it slowly, then continue adding the remaining oil.

Once you are familiar with the basic method of making mayonnaise you can experiment with different oils and vinegars as seasonings. There are countless variations of the basic recipe. Here are a few of them.

AÏOLI OR GARLIC MAYONNAISE

Crush a couple of cloves of garlic and add them to the basic recipe. This is delicious with cold poached crayfish or on a crouton in fish soups.

AVOCADO MAYONNAISE

Beat an avocado to a paste and add it to the basic recipe. Season with lemon and a pinch of cayenne pepper and serve it with lightly poached scallops and crudités.

FRESH HERB MAYONNAISE

Season the mayonnaise with a little garlic and finely chopped fresh herbs. The choice of herbs depends on your preference. You can use just one herb (for example, dill) or a combination, and the strength of the herb flavour should be to your own taste. Avoid rosemary and sage as they have no affinity with mayonnaise.

MUSTARD MAYONNAISE

To the basic recipe add 2 tb French wholegrain mustard. Taste and season.

SAUCE RÉMOULADE

This is a superior tartare sauce and can be used with most grilled fish.

> **3 anchovy fillets finely chopped**
> **1 tb capers**
> **1 tb gherkins chopped**
> **1 tb French mustard**
> **$1/2$ tb tarragon chopped**
> **$1/2$ tb parsley chopped**

Combine all the ingredients well and add to the basic recipe.

MAYONNAISE WITH KINA

Take the corals from 4 sea urchins, or kina, drain them well and beat them to a rough paste with a fork. Fold them into the mayonnaise and season with a little lemon juice and chopped parsley. Good in fish soups and stews.

Butters

Savoury butters liven up almost every kind of barbecued, grilled or fried fish. They are quick to make and, if formed into a cylinder and wrapped in tin foil, can be kept in the freezer until needed.

FRESH HERB BUTTER

> **200 g soft butter**
> **100 g mixed fresh herbs (garlic, parsley, tarragon, chives, chervil, dill, for example, but not rosemary or sage as these two will dominate)**
> **salt and black pepper**

Put all ingredients into a food processor and whisk until the mixture is creamy. Form into a cylinder and wrap in tin foil. Keep very cold until needed, then simply cut off as many slices as you need. Using this basic recipe, you can experiment with combinations of herbs or make butters using only your favourite herb.

ALMOND BUTTER

> **100 g unblanched almonds**
> **200 g butter**
> **salt, pepper and lemon juice for seasoning**

Roast the almonds and roughly grind them. Beat them into the butter until creamy. Season with salt, pepper and lemon juice.
Experiment using other nuts to make a variation of this butter. Hazelnuts, macadamias and pecans are delicious alternatives.

CRAYFISH BUTTER

> 200 g butter
> 200 g crayfish meat, finely chopped, including
> the coral and creamy parts of the crayfish
> salt and pepper

Beat all ingredients until smooth.

SMOKED SALMON BUTTER

> 200 g butter
> 100 g smoked salmon
> lemon juice and black pepper for seasoning

Cream butter and salmon, then add seasonings.

MUSTARD BUTTER

> 200 g butter
> 2 tb wholegrain French mustard

Beat the butter and mustard together until creamy.

LIME BUTTER

> 200 g butter
> 1 tsp chives chopped
> 1/4 tsp ginger finely chopped
> juice and zest of 1 lime

Beat all ingredients until creamy.

ANISE BUTTER

200 g butter
1 tsp parsley chopped
4 tb Pernod, pastis or ouzo

Combine butter and parsley, then beat in the spirits.

Sauce hollandaise and variations, for plainly cooked fish and seafood

A sauce deluxe, easy to master and always impressive. The method described here is the one most frequently used by busy chefs. It is fast and avoids most of the pitfalls of the traditional method. The result is just as good, if not better.

Sauce hollandaise is like mayonnaise, except that melted butter instead of oil is added to the egg yolks to make the emulsion. The consistency of the finished sauce is like lightly whipped cream, and its colour is an appetising golden yellow.

250 g unsalted butter
juice of half a lemon
1 tb white wine
3 egg yolks

Gently melt the butter and put to one side.

Put the next three ingredients into a large metal bowl, and place the bowl over a saucepan of hot, but not boiling water. Whisk over the heat until the egg yolks are pale and frothy. They will almost double in bulk.

Take the yolk mixture off the heat and whisk in the melted butter, a little at a time, as you would the oil for mayonnaise.

Season with ground white pepper and salt.

Keep the sauce warm if you are not using it immediately. Direct heat or cold draughts will make the sauce turn, always a problem with butter sauces.

If this should happen, put the turned sauce over gentle heat and let it melt and separate completely. Take a clean bowl and into it put a few tablespoons of boiling water. Add the melted sauce to the boiling water, whisking all the time, and voilà! Your sauce will have revived.

SAUCE BÉARNAISE

The classical sauce beloved of chefs for grilled meat. It is delicious with the meatier types of fish like hapuku, tuna cooked medium rare or thick fillets of snapper, grilled and served with fresh green salad and french bread.

Béarnaise is identical to hollandaise in its making, but it has a different flavour.

Instead of flavouring the sauce with lemon and wine, use the following reduction (a mixture reduced in volume by boiling).

> **6 tb white wine**
> **6 tb white vinegar or, better still, tarragon wine vinegar**
> **1 tb shallot chopped (an onion will do if shallots are not available)**
> **2 or 3 parsley stalks**
> **black pepper and a pinch of salt**
> **2 tb tarragon chopped**

Put all ingredients into a saucepan, bring to the boil and cook carefully until the mixture is reduced to half its original volume. Cool completely.

Melt the butter as for the basic recipe for hollandaise sauce.

Put the reduction into the bowl with the egg yolks and proceed according to the recipe for hollandaise.

When the sauce is made, finish it with 1 tb chopped tarragon and parsley. Adjust the seasonings.

SAUCE VERTE (GREEN SAUCE)

Make the basic hollandaise recipe (page 26) and add the following:

1 tb fresh tarragon very finely chopped
1 tb parsley very finely chopped
1 tb chervil very finely chopped
5 or 6 spinach leaves lightly cooked in boiling,
salted water, dried well, cooled and chopped to a
purée
a little lemon juice, pepper and salt for seasoning

CUCUMBER AND DILL HOLLANDAISE

Make the basic hollandaise recipe (see page 26).

1 tb fresh dill
half a telegraph cucumber
salt

Cut the cucumber into thin slices.

Liberally sprinkle it with salt and leave it for half an hour. This will make any bitterness disappear and soften it.

Rinse off all the salt with plenty of cold water and squeeze dry. Chop it almost to a purée.

Chop the fresh dill finely. Add the cucumber and dill to the basic hollandaise recipe.

Taste the sauce and adjust the seasoning.

This sauce is excellent with salmon or poached white fish.

ARTICHOKE HOLLANDAISE

Make the basic hollandaise recipe (see page 26).

5 or 6 artichoke hearts
lemon juice

Thinly slice the freshly boiled (and cooled) artichoke hearts and add them to the basic sauce recipe. Season with extra lemon juice. Tinned artichoke hearts can be used, although their flavour is not quite as good.

Other sauces

FRESH TOMATO SAUCE

A quick fresh-tasting sauce which relies on the taste of good quality tomatoes for its appeal.

> 100 ml olive oil
> 2 cloves garlic finely chopped
> 5 or 6 tomatoes cored, peeled by submerging them in boiling water for 20 seconds, then roughly chopped
> 3 basil leaves
> black pepper, salt and sugar

In a large frying pan, heat the oil until hot but not smoking. Add the garlic and let it cook for 1 minute.

Add the tomatoes and stirfry for 2 minutes. Tear up the basil leaves and add them to the sauce.

Take off the heat and add the seasonings.

Do not cook this sauce for more than 2 or 3 minutes. The charm of the sauce is in the incredibly fresh taste of the tomatoes, which is lost entirely if the sauce is overcooked.

A few chopped anchovy fillets, thrown in at the last moment, are an added bonus.

Makes about 2 cups.

FRESH COCONUT CHUTNEY

Based on a recipe from *Prashad, Cooking with the Indian Masters* (Bombay 1986)

> 100 g freshly grated or desiccated coconut
> $1^1/_2$ cups coriander leaves
> 2 fresh hot green chillis
> 3 cloves garlic

> 1 tb coriander seeds toasted and ground finely
> 2 tb cumin seeds toasted and ground finely
> 1/2 cup lime juice
> 2 tb sugar
> 1 cup coconut cream

Put everything into the food processor and process to a thick paste.

Use this chutney as it is as an accompaniment to barbecued, grilled or lightly panfried fish or seafood, or use it to stuff a whole fish which is then wrapped in banana leaves or oiled foil and baked, or spread it over boneless, skinned white fish fillets which are then wrapped in banana leaves or oiled foil and steamed.

Makes about 2 cups.

VINAIGRETTE

In France vinaigrette is regarded as a sauce, not merely a salad dressing. Use the best olive oil you can find, preferably extra virgin olive oil as it is an unrectified, natural product.

Use wine or cider vinegar, if using vinegar, or fresh lemon juice.

Do not mistake a lack of flavour for too little vinegar or lemon juice since while vinaigrette must have the acidity provided by vinegar or lemon juice, it also needs to be seasoned well to bring out the taste combination of the oil and vinegar/lemon juice.

> 5 parts olive oil to 1 part vinegar or lemon juice,
> or a mixture of the two
> crushed garlic, pepper and salt to flavour and
> season.

Just how much of the acid components (the vinegar or lemon juice and the garlic) you use depends on your own taste.

Vinaigrettes can be made with lime juice, have fresh chopped green herbs added, be flavoured with mustards, capers, chopped gherkins, chilli, the list goes on.

Once you understand how the oil/acidic combination works, experiment with other of your favourite tastes and combinations.

Vinaigrette is good with most plainly barbecued, grilled or panfried fish and seafood.

VIETNAMESE DIPPING SAUCE — NUOC CHAM

This is the hot sour dipping sauce which one sees at almost every meal in Vietnam.

Barbecued, grilled or panfried fish or seafood, with a bowl of Nuoc Cham, rice or noodles and plenty of sliced cucumber, tomato, bean sprouts, salad greens and sprigs of fresh herbs (mint, coriander, basil and dill) can turn eating the day's catch into a trip to Saigon.

> 1/4 cup fish sauce (nuoc mam)
> 1 large clove garlic finely chopped
> 1 fresh red chilli finely sliced
> 3 tb lime juice
> 2 tb sugar

Mix well until the sugar dissolves and let stand 30 minutes for the flavours to combine.

Makes 1 cup.

Like most South-east Asian food, this sauce combines hot, sweet, salty and sour tastes and these can be adjusted to suit oneself; just add more of the ingredient that appeals to your taste.

This sauce can also be varied with one of the following: the juice squeezed from grated fresh ginger, a dash of light soy sauce, a little tamarind paste, finely grated shredded carrot and daikon (white radish), chopped coriander stalks, chopped mint or Vietnamese mint.

ELIZABETH DAVID'S SAUCE MESSINE

Tarragon, chervil and parsley are the essential herbs in this delicious cream sauce, which comes from Lorraine. I have used this recipe again and again, both as part of restaurant cookery and at home, always with gratifying results. Good with plainly cooked fish and seafood.

6 sprigs tarragon
6 sprigs chervil
6 sprigs parsley
2 small shallots
50 g butter
1 tsp flour
1 tsp French mustard
2 egg yolks beaten
300 ml cream
salt and pepper
lemon juice

Finely chop the tarragon, chervil, parsley and shallots.
Mix together the butter and flour and add the mustard, beaten egg yolks and cream. Stir in the herb and shallot mixture and season with salt and pepper.
Put the mixture into a metal bowl and stand it in a saucepan of hot water. Heat gently, stirring all the time until the sauce thickens. Do not boil. Add the juice of a small lemon just before serving.
Makes 1 $^1/_2$ - 2 cups.

SPICE PASTE

This spiced roasted tomato and capsicum 'paste' is good with fried, grilled, barbecued and poached fish or seafood or as an accompaniment to seafood soups and stews.

> 2 tomatoes, cored and roasted with a little olive oil in a 200°C oven until browned and collapsing
> 1 red capsicum roasted over a flame or grilled until blackened, skinned, seeded and cored
> 1/2 cup almonds roasted and chopped
> 3 cloves garlic chopped
> 1 tb paprika
> 2 tb each of cumin seeds and coriander seeds, roasted and ground to a powder
> 2 tb dried red chilli chopped
> 1/2 tsp brown sugar
> salt to taste

Process everything to a smooth purée in a food processor. Season with the salt.

Makes 1-1 1/2 cups depending on the size of the tomatoes and capsicum.

PESTO

The famous basil cream from Genoa. It is usually eaten with pasta, but it is especially good with lightly poached scallops or crayfish.

> 2 cups fresh basil leaves
> 2 cloves garlic
> 25 g pine nuts
> 25 g of grated parmesan cheese
> 50 ml olive oil
> salt and pepper for seasoning

Blend the first four ingredients to a paste. With the blender still running, add the olive oil, a little at a time, as for mayonnaise. Season to taste. The sauce should be thick and creamy and a vivid green.

Makes 1 cup.

ROUILLE

> 1 large, red capsicum
> 1 large clove garlic
> 1 dried red chilli
> 1 cup breadcrumbs
> 100 ml olive oil
> fish stock (optional)
> salt and pepper

Grill, or burn over a flame, the skin of the capsicum, until it is black and charred. Wash off the burnt skin under running water and discard the core and seeds.

Put the capsicum into a food processor or blender with the garlic, chilli and a handful of breadcrumbs that have been soaked in water and then squeezed dry. Blend to a paste, then continue blending while adding the olive oil, a little at a time, as for mayonnaise.

Thin with a little fish stock if a runnier sauce is required. Taste and season with salt and pepper.

Use this coral-coloured cream as an accompaniment to fish soups and stews, or like a savoury butter with poached, grilled or fried fish.

Makes 1 $^1/_2$ - 2 cups.

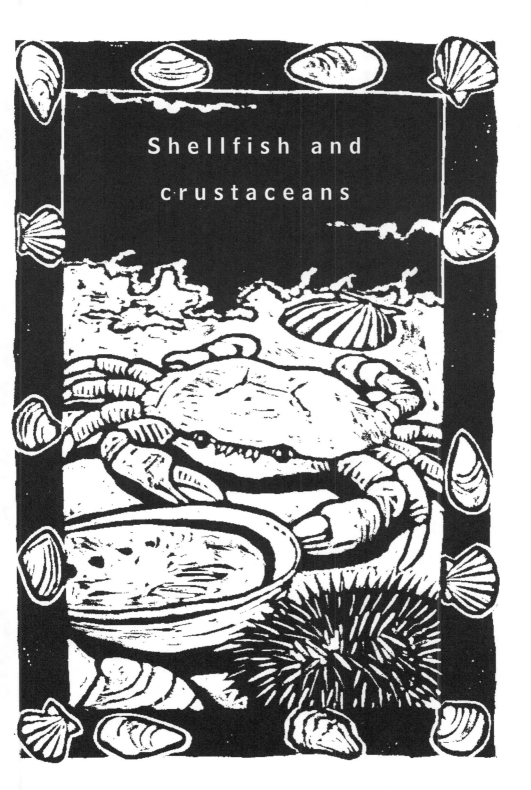

Shellfish and crustaceans

Mussels

Always use mussels live.

The shells must be tightly shut or close when given a sharp tap. If they do not close, throw them away, together with any that are cracked or broken.

Scrub live mussels well in clean water and pull out the beards. It is prudent to use them the day you buy (or collect) them. They will last only a day or two in a cool place, and refrigerators are generally too cold, killing them rather quickly, making storage tricky and not recommended.

MUSSELS WITH TOMATOES AND SALAMI
(Based on a recipe by Elizabeth David)

2 dozen medium-sized mussels scrubbed and
debearded
100 ml olive oil
3 cloves garlic finely chopped
1 small onion finely chopped
$^1/_2$ cup white wine
400 g tin Italian whole peeled tomatoes in juice,
mashed
1 tsp sugar
$^1/_2$ cup spicy salami diced 1 cm
1 small iceberg or cos lettuce sliced
salt and pepper
black olives
chopped parsley

Heat the oil over moderate heat in a large saucepan. Add the
onions and garlic and stirfry, without browning, until soft.
Add the mussels, wine, sugar, tomatoes and salami. Stirfry until
the mussels open, removing them as they do to a serving platter.
Add the lettuce to the pan, bring to the boil and mix well.
Taste and season with salt and pepper.
Pour the sauce around the mussels and garnish with black olives
and chopped parsley.
Serves four.

MUSSELS STEAMED WITH VEGETABLES

250 g butter
1 handful sorrel (150 g) chopped
2 tb parsley chopped
2 cloves garlic crushed
2 potatoes cut into 2 cm dice
1 carrot cut into 2 cm dice
1 stick of celery thinly sliced
1 small bunch spinach washed and chopped
1 onion chopped finely
2 courgettes sliced
1 tb ham finely chopped
200 ml dry white wine
black pepper
3 dozen small live mussels

In a large pot, melt the butter. Add the herbs, vegetables and ham. Fry gently, without browning, so that the vegetables are hot and coated with butter. Add the wine and a few turns of pepper from a pepper grinder. Turn the heat well down and let the mixture fry or, rather, sweat for 10 minutes, until the potatoes and carrots are cooked.

Add the mussels, put on the lid and turn the heat up. Cook until the mussels open, removing them as they do. Put them onto a hot serving dish and pile the vegetables around them. Serve immediately.

Enough for four.

MUSSELS STEAMED WITH ONIONS AND HERBS

100 g butter
4 onions sliced
2 cloves garlic crushed
3 tb parsley chopped
2 tb mixed fresh herbs (eg Italian parsley, thyme
leaves, chervil, marjoram, bay, dill) chopped
100 ml dry white wine or cider
3 dozen small live mussels

Melt the butter in a large saucepan and add the onions and herbs. Let them get hot, stirring with a wooden spoon. Turn down the heat and very gently fry the mixture for 8 to 10 minutes or until the onions are soft and golden. Pour in the wine or cider and bring to the boil. Add the mussels, put on the lid and steam them open. Remove the mussels to a hot serving dish as they open and pile the onions around them.

Serves four.

WARM MUSSEL AND POTATO SALAD

4 waxy potatoes
2 dozen mussels cooked in a little water, shelled
and sliced
2 sticks of celery sliced thinly
2 spring onions finely sliced
1 tb parsley chopped
2 tb capers
2 tomatoes, core removed, diced into 2 cm cubes
1 cup well-seasoned mayonnaise (see page 20)

Scrub the potatoes and cut them into large, bite-sized pieces. Boil them in salted water until they are cooked but firm. They must not be overcooked.

When the potatoes are cooked, drain them well and put them in a salad bowl while they are still hot. Quickly add all the other ingredients except the tomatoes. Give the salad a few careful turns to mix it. Sprinkle the tomatoes over the top. On top of this, sprinkle some more chopped parsley. The heat of the potatoes will warm the salad and develop the flavours.

A good lunch for four.

MOULES À LA CRÈME

An old-fashioned French way of serving mussels.

2 egg yolks
300 ml cream
100 g butter
1 shallot chopped very finely
1 small carrot and 1 small stick of celery cut into
$^1/_2$ cm dice
2 tb parsley chopped
100 ml dry white wine or cider
3 dozen small mussels scrubbed and beards
removed
black pepper, lemon juice

Beat the egg yolks in 100 ml of the cream.

In a heavy saucepan melt the butter over a gentle heat. Add the vegetables and the parsley. Stirfry gently for 2 or 3 minutes without browning.

Add the wine and mussels, cover the pan and let them steam open in the usual way. When they have opened, remove them to a hot serving dish and keep them warm.

Bring the liquid in the saucepan to the boil and add the cream. Boil until the liquid has reduced by a quarter. Take off the boil and whisk in the egg yolk mixture. This will enrich and thicken the sauce. Do not boil the sauce again once the egg yolks have been added or it will curdle.

Taste the sauce and season it with the pepper and lemon juice then pour it over the mussels.

Serve with crusty bread.

Serves four.

MUSSELS STEAMED WITH OLIVE OIL AND THYME

Perhaps the simplest and most delicious way of preparing mussels.

**3 dozen medium-sized mussels scrubbed and debearded
2 cloves garlic crushed
2 large sprigs of fresh thyme
100 ml extra virgin olive oil
freshly ground black pepper**

Put everything into a large saucepan, cover and place over high heat. Cook, giving the pan an occasional shake, until the mussels have steamed open, removing them as they do so they do not overcook.

Put the mussels into a large serving bowl and pour over the olive oil mixture that remains in the pan.

Serve with crusty bread.

Serves four.

MUSSELS WITH ASIAN GREENS AND EGG NOODLES

100 ml vegetable oil
2 cloves garlic finely chopped
12 mussels scrubbed and debearded
3 cups mixed Asian greens that have been quickly wilted in boiling water, refreshed under cold water and squeezed dry (any combination or one of the following are suitable: baby bok choy, ong choy, choy sum, gai lan or failing that, spinach, watercress, young silverbeet, cabbage, or broccoli florets)
4 spring onions sliced into 5 cm lengths
$1/4$ cup coriander stalks and leaves chopped
3 cups cooked thick Chinese egg noodles (precook in plenty of boiling water, refresh under cold water and drain well)
3 tb fish sauce
soy sauce

Heat the oil in a wok until hot but not smoking. Add the garlic, mussels, spring onions and greens.

Turn the heat up and stirfry until the mussels have opened.

Add the coriander, noodles and fish sauce and stirfry until the noodles are hot.

Serve with soy sauce on the side to be added by each person if desired.

Serves two to four.

MUSSEL BOUILLON

3 dozen fresh mussels scrubbed and debearded
50 ml olive oil
1 small onion finely chopped
1 clove garlic finely chopped
1 tb parsley chopped
100 ml dry white wine
1 litre well-flavoured fish stock

GARNISH
3 tomatoes cored, peeled and seeded
slices of french bread that have been painted with
olive oil and baked until crisp and golden in a hot
oven
6 tb aïoli (garlic mayonnaise) (see page 21)

Put the mussels into a pot with 3 cm of water in the bottom of it.
Put the lid on it and bring to the boil over a fast heat.
When the water is boiling, remove the lid and, as each mussel opens and shrinks away from the shell, take it out and let it cool.
When all the mussels have opened, strain the cooking liquid and set aside to cool.
Take the mussels out of their shells and mince them finely.
Heat the oil over moderate heat. Add the onion and garlic and cook

for a few minutes. Add the minced mussels and parsley and let them start to bubble. Stir them with a wooden spoon to prevent sticking.

Add the wine, cook for 2 minutes then add the stock and 100 ml of the liquid in which the mussels were cooked.

Bring to the boil and simmer for 10 minutes. Taste and season with salt and pepper.

This is a light, thin soup. If you want a stronger flavour add more of the mussel liquid and cut out most of the salt in the seasoning as the mussel liquid tends to be quite salty.

Serve the soup with a round slice of french bread in the middle of a plate. On top of the bread put a generous spoonful of aïoli, and over this sprinkle some chopped raw tomato and more chopped parsley.

Serves four to six.

MUSSEL, SORREL, POTATO AND LEEK SOUP

A word about sorrel. Its botanical name is Rumex scutatus *and it looks like the young leaves from the middle of a bunch of spinach. It can be used like spinach as a purée or like a herb as a flavouring. It is easy to grow; just plant seeds or seedlings in some reasonable soil that gets some sun, and it will look after itself. My sorrel has been growing in the same patch for about four years and all I do is pick it.*

Sorrel makes an excellent standby for omelette fillings, soups and, especially, sauces for fish. Its tangy flavour is the perfect foil for fish.

3 dozen mussels which have been steamed open
in a little water (reserve the liquid)
200 g butter
2 medium potatoes finely diced
1 leek thinly sliced
1 onion finely chopped
1 clove garlic finely chopped
1 tb parsley chopped
100 ml dry white wine
500 ml water
150 g (or 1 large handful) sorrel finely sliced
300 ml cream
salt and pepper

Slice the mussels thinly and put them to one side.

In a saucepan melt the butter over a gentle heat and add the veg-etables, garlic and parsley, but not the sorrel. Cook the vegetables gently for 5 minutes, being careful not to brown them. Add the sliced mussels and stir gently with a wooden spoon. Add the wine and let the mixture boil for a few moments.

Strain the mussel liquid through a fine sieve and add a third of it to the contents of the saucepan. Pour in the water and bring it back to the boil. Add the sorrel and simmer until the vegetables are soft.

Add the cream, taste and season with salt and pepper. Do not boil the soup once the cream has been added as it could curdle.

The soup can be left like this — a hearty soup with plenty of veg-etables visible — or it can be blended in a food processor for a finer result. The choice is yours.

Serves four for lunch.

MUSSEL, CORN AND BACON SOUP

12 medium-sized mussels scrubbed and
debearded
1 sprig parsley
2 bay leaves
2 cloves garlic finely chopped
1 cup dry white wine

Put everything into a saucepan and bring to the boil. Cover and let the mussels steam open.

Remove from the heat and when the mussels are cool enough to handle remove them from the liquid, shell them, chop them coarsely and set aside. Strain the liquid and reserve.

4 tb olive oil
3 rashers rindless bacon diced
2 waxy potatoes peeled and diced
1 onion peeled and chopped
2 cups fish stock
1 cup whole kernel corn drained
3 tb Italian parsley chopped
1 cup cream

Heat the oil in a large saucepan over moderate heat. Add the bacon, potatoes and onion and stirfry 5 minutes without browning. Add the stock, mussel liquid and the corn and simmer 10 minutes until the potatoes are cooked.

Stir in the chopped mussels, parsley and cream and bring back to the boil.

Taste and season with salt if necessary and freshly ground black pepper.

Serves four to six.

SEAFOOD SOUP WITH SPICE PASTE

4 tb olive oil
1 clove garlic finely chopped
2 bay leaves
1 onion chopped
$1/2$ tsp fennel seeds
400 g tin Italian whole peeled tomatoes in juice,
mashed
500 ml fish stock
8 small mussels scrubbed and debearded
300 g non-oily white fish, skinned, boned, diced
into 4 cm pieces
10 tuatua scrubbed
10 scallops sliced
Italian parsley
salt and pepper

In a heavy saucepan, heat the oil over moderate heat. Add the garlic, onion, bay, fennel, and stirfry until the onion is soft and golden. Add the tomatoes and stock and bring to the boil, mixing well.

Add the mussels and tuatua and simmer until they open. Bring to the boil and add the fish and scallops. Bring back to the boil.

Taste and season with salt and pepper. Sprinkle with plenty of roughly chopped Italian parsley and serve with the spice paste (see page 34) on the side.

Each person helps themselves to a spoonful of spice paste to top the soup.

Serves four to six.

SHELLFISH AND CRUSTACEANS

CHILLED COCONUT AND SEAFOOD SOUP

THE MUSSELS

12 medium sized mussels scrubbed and
debearded
1 tb ginger finely sliced
1 tb lemongrass, white bulbous ends only, finely
sliced
2 cloves garlic finely chopped
$1/2$ cup water

Mix everything well in a large saucepan, put on high heat and steam the mussels open. Remove the mussels, cool and slice. Set aside. Strain the liquid and reserve.

THE SQUID AND FISH

1 squid tube, opened out flat and scored in a grid
pattern on the outside, cut into small bite sized
pieces, dropped into boiling water for 30 seconds
until just cooked through, well drained and
refreshed under cold water to stop it cooking
300 g firm white skinned boned fish fillet or
fresh tuna sliced thinly

MARINADE
4 tb fish sauce
4 tb lime juice
2 tsp sugar
1 green chilli or more if desired, finely sliced

Mix the raw fish and the blanched squid with the marinade and set aside 30 minutes.

THE SOUP

1 cup reserved mussel liquid
200 ml coconut cream
450 ml fish or chicken stock
1 clove garlic finely chopped
2 tb each coriander, mint and basil leaves
2 tomatoes cored, seeded and diced
1 cup seeded cucumber diced
1/2 red capsicum cored, seeded and diced
1 tb fish sauce
zest and juice of 2 limes
100 g glass (also called cellophane or beanthread) noodles, soaked 30 minutes in hot water, cooked until transparent in boiling water, cooled under cold water and drained well

Mix everything together in a large bowl.

Add the mussels, squid and fish and their marinade. Toss gently.

Taste and season with extra fish sauce, lime juice and sugar if necessary. The soup should have a pleasant sweet/sour/hot flavour.

Cover and place in the refrigerator until completely chilled.

Serves six as a first course or four as a main dish with extra noodles.

STEAMED SEAFOOD WITH SOBA NOODLES AND GREENS

This is a favourite recipe which is based on one from Shizuo Tsuji's definitive book Japanese Cooking, A Simple Art *(Kodansha International 1980).*

You need a large bamboo steamer or large baking tray of boiling water in a hot oven for this dish.

Any combination of seafood is excellent cooked this way, as are skinned, boned salmon fillets by themselves. It makes a stunning first course to a dinner party and can be assembled in advance and cooked when needed.

6 scallops halved
300 g snapper
1 small raw crayfish tail sliced into 6 slices
12 shucked oysters
100 g green tea noodles (cha-soba) cooked al dente in plenty of boiling water, refreshed in cold water to stop them cooking and drained well
6 pieces dried giant kelp (Konbu) 2 cm long (for flavouring and not to be eaten)
sake
6 very small baby bok choy leaves and 6 small spinach leaves wilted quickly in boiling water and squeezed dry
6 pieces spring onion 2 cm long
1 sheet nori (the seaweed sheets used to wrap sushi) toasted by passing through a low gas flame or over a low electric element, then shredded

SAUCE

2 cups fish stock
100 ml mirin (sweet rice wine)
100 ml Japanese soy sauce
1 cup dried bonito flakes

Bring stock, mirin and soy sauce to the boil. Add
the bonito flakes and strain immediately or it will
become bitter. Discard the bonito flakes.
Keep hot until needed.

Assemble 6 small bowls, teacups or ramekins.

Put a piece of konbu into the bottom of each and a small mound of cha-soba on top.

Put 1 piece of each seafood into each bowl.

Add 1 bok choy and 1 spinach leaf to each bowl with a piece of spring onion.

Lightly sprinkle with sake but do not drown the seafood.

Cover tightly with plastic wrap or foil and steam over high heat for 15 minutes or put into a baking dish of boiling water into a preheated oven at 200°C.

Uncover and top with a liberal amount of the hot sauce.

Garnish with the nori.

Serves six.

Crayfish

(ALSO CALLED ROCK LOBSTER)

There are many grand and complicated recipes for crayfish but as it is such a luxury it seems absurd to mask its flavour with too many ingredients. The flavour of frozen or precooked crayfish is disappointing and is best avoided. If you are lucky enough to get your hands on freshly caught crayfish, treat it simply.

Split down the middle as in the following recipe, the flesh well brushed with garlic-flavoured olive oil and put flesh-side down onto a hot barbecue is one of my favourite ways of dealing with a live crayfish. Bread, salad and a glass of wine are the only necessary accompaniments.

CRAYFISH GRILLED WITH HERB BUTTER
AND SAUCE ROUILLE

**1 live crayfish
herb butter (see pages 23-25)
Pernod (optional)**

Hold the crayfish with a thick cloth to protect your hand and using
a heavy, sharp knife, split the crayfish down the middle, starting at
the head, to form 2 identical pieces of raw crayfish in the shell.
Make a herb butter with your favourite fresh herbs.
Lie the crayfish pieces shell side down on a fireproof dish and liberally dot the flesh with pieces of herb butter.
Heat the grill, put the crayfish under it and grill until it is cooked,
being careful it does not burn. It is cooked when you can pierce the
flesh easily with a knife and the knife comes out cleanly.
Serve with a green salad, french bread and sauce rouille (see page
35).
A few teaspoons of Pernod sprinkled over the crayfish with the
herb butter is a delicious variation.
Serves two.

CRAYFISH WITH AÏOLI AND CRUDITÉS

One of the most pleasing and impressive hors d'oeuvres is a plainly boiled crayfish served cool (but not icy cold) with plenty of french bread, aïoli or garlic mayonnaise (see page 21) and raw vegetables.

The vegetables can simply be carrot and celery sticks, spring onions and blanched broccoli, or crudités of a more deluxe variety: artichoke hearts, marinated mushrooms or asparagus. Each is perfect in its own way as a foil for the richness of the crayfish and mayonnaise.

Heap everything onto your biggest serving dish. Make sure it is all fresh looking and naturally arranged, then present it at the table. The reaction is always gratifying.

CRAYFISH AND TOMATO SOUP

This is a very simple soup. It is a vegetable purée with fish stock and crayfish added. So many crayfish bisques contain tomatoes for colour yet remain nondescript in flavour. Here the tomato is elevated alongside the crayfish to make a soup with an honest tomato and crayfish flavour.

4 tb olive oil
1 carrot, 1 small leek, 1 small onion, 2 cloves garlic, all chopped
1 sprig thyme
half a bay leaf
300 g tomatoes cored, peeled and seeded
1 tb tomato paste
1 tsp sugar
1 litre fish stock

1 medium-sized raw crayfish (1–1.5 kg)
pepper and salt
butter
cream and parsley for garnishing

Heat the oil in the bottom of a heavy saucepan until it is almost smoking. Add the carrot, leek, onion and herbs. Let them brown, stirring occasionally so they do not stick.

Add the chopped tomatoes, tomato purée and sugar. Bring to the boil and add the stock. Cover the pan and simmer for 20 minutes. While the soup is simmering, split the crayfish down the middle with a sharp knife. Cut straight through the shell to make two identical halves. Remove the tail meat and cut into slices 1 cm thick. Crack the legs, remove the meat. Set the meat aside.

After the soup has simmered and the vegetables are cooked, remove the bay leaf and the thyme and purée the soup.

Taste and season it, put it back on the heat and bring it to the boil. When it reaches boiling point add the crayfish meat. The soup will stop boiling, so let it come to the boil again, by which time the crayfish will have cooked.

Take it off the heat and stir in a generous knob of butter.

Serve immediately.

Serves four as an entrée or light lunch.

GAZPACHO WITH CRAYFISH

A luxury dish for a summer dinner party. Gazpacho is like a liquid salad. This recipe is a combination of tastes, hardly original, but highly successful with family and friends.
Buy (or catch) a medium-sized crayfish; these days a medium one would weigh about 1–1.5 kg.
A raw crayfish that you cook yourself has an infinitely better flavour and texture than one bought precooked because it is alive up until the time you cook it. However, a precooked crayfish will do for this recipe if nothing else is available. Since they cost so much, it is worth interrogating your fishmonger as to when the crayfish was cooked and for how long.

PREPARING THE CRAYFISH
Assuming you have a live crayfish, this is how to deal with it:
Poach it whole in salted water. There are two schools of thought on the kindest way to kill a crayfish. You can either plunge it into the boiling, salted water, and it will be all over in seconds, or you can put it into cold, salted water (with a weighted lid so that it cannot jump out) and bring it to the boil. Apparently it goes to sleep, for ever, at 26˚C. It is entirely up to you which method you choose.
Once the water is boiling, simmer the crayfish for 10 minutes for each kilo of its weight. When the crayfish is cooked, remove it from the pot and submerge it in cold water to stop further cooking.
Let it cool, then detach the tail from the body (the legs can be set aside and used in a salad). Slit the underside of the shell with a knife or kitchen shears, being careful not to cut into the meat. Pull the shell away from the meat so that the meat comes out intact. Slice the meat finely, making thin lozenges of crayfish, white in the middle, edged with pink. Set these aside.

THE GAZPACHO

6 tomatoes peeled and chopped almost to a purée
1 red capsicum finely diced
3 spring onions finely sliced
1 telegraph cucumber seeds removed, finely diced.
3 cloves garlic finely chopped
2 tb mixed fresh herbs (basil, parsley, chives, marjoram are good choices) finely chopped
a few black olives
150 ml olive oil
50 ml wine vinegar
1/2 litre cold water
black pepper and salt

Put the herbs and the vegetables into a large serving bowl.
Mix the oil and the vinegar thoroughly and pour over the vegetables. Add the water and mix well. Put into the refrigerator to chill for 2 or 3 hours. This allows the flavour to develop. Take the soup out of the refrigerator and taste and season well. Add the crayfish slices and mix them carefully into the soup.
Serve with ice in the soup and brown bread on the side.
Enough for four.

Crab

CRAB OMELETTE

1 kg live paddle crabs
2 large onions thinly sliced
50 g butter plus extra to fry the omelette
1 tb parsley chopped
6 or 7 eggs

Wash the paddle crabs well and cook in boiling, salted water for 10 minutes.

Cool them, crack the shells and legs (they are quite soft) and remove the meat. Set it to one side.

Fry the onions gently in the butter until they are golden but not browned. Set aside.

Melt some more butter in a large frying pan (a 25–30 cm pan is a good size) and make a large omelette out of the eggs, which have been beaten very briefly with a fork.

When the bottom of the omelette is cooked but the top is still runny, spread the onions over it. Spread the crab meat on top of the onions and sprinkle with the parsley. Fold the omelette in half and turn it out onto a warm plate.

Excellent for lunch. Enough for two or three people when served with salad.

POTTED CRAB

5 live paddle crabs boiled for 10 minutes in salted water
300 g butter
25 ml dry white wine
1 clove garlic crushed
1 tb parsley chopped
pinch of nutmeg
pinch of cayenne pepper
salt and pepper
juice of 1 lemon

Remove the meat from the crabs and crumble it into small pieces. Put all the ingredients into a saucepan over a gentle heat and stir slowly until the butter has melted. Cook a further 2 minutes, being careful the butter does not brown at all. Taste and season with the salt and pepper. Pour into a deep earthenware dish and refrigerate.

When the mixture has set, serve spread on hot toast.

CREAM OF CRAB AND CUCUMBER SOUP

For this recipe try to use the large paddle crabs that are often available from good fishshops. A quarter of their body weight is meat and it is easy to extract because their shells are quite soft. If you catch the crabs yourself they will probably be smaller and require a little more patience as you will need about double the number given in this recipe. However, you will be rewarded when you taste the soup. It is excellent.

$1^1/_2$ litres light chicken stock
10 large crabs
50 g butter
1 tb each chopped dill and parsley
1 clove garlic chopped finely
1 small onion chopped finely
50 g flour
50 ml dry white wine
1 large telegraph cucumber seeds removed
chopped roughly
100 ml cream
juice of 1 lemon
salt and pepper

Put the stock into a large saucepan and bring it to the boil. Add the crabs (you might have to do this in batches if they will not all fit in at once), cover and bring to the boil again. Simmer for 10 minutes, until the crabs are cooked. Remove the crabs and let them cool. Strain the stock and reserve it.

When the crabs are cool enough to handle, crack them open (you can do this with your hands, the shells are quite soft) and remove the meat.

In a heavy saucepan melt the butter over a gentle heat so that it does not burn. Add the herbs, garlic and onion and fry gently for 2 or 3 minutes, making sure the onion does not colour.

Add the flour and stir well. Take it off the heat and pour in the wine, stirring all the time. Add the cucumber, then the stock and continue stirring.

Put the pan back on the heat, add the crab meat and bring to the boil. Simmer until the cucumber is soft, then purée in the blender. Add the cream, taste the soup and season it with salt, pepper and the lemon juice.

Serves four to six.

CRAB SALAD

5 paddle crabs (or catch some of the big crabs
that you see sliding under rocks at the beach if
you have the patience; they have plenty of meat
and flavour)
250 g rice
2 hardboiled eggs cut into wedges
100 g toasted almonds roughly chopped
1 red capsicum cut into 2 cm dice
1 gherkin sliced thinly
2 spring onions chopped thinly
1 stick celery sliced thinly
1 tb parsley chopped
2 tomatoes cut into thin wedges
150 ml vinaigrette made from 6 parts olive oil to
1 part wine vinegar, well seasoned with salt and
pepper and a clove of crushed garlic

Cook the crabs in boiling, salted water for 10 minutes. When they are cool, remove the meat and set it aside.

Next cook the rice. You must use an equal amount of rice and water (ie 1 bowl of rice to the same bowl of water), so measure the rice, wash it and drain it well. Put the rice into a saucepan and put in the equal amount of water. Bring it to the boil, then turn the heat down as far as possible. Cover the saucepan tightly and set the timer for exactly 20 minutes. Do not lift the lid for any reason as the rice is steaming. After 20 minutes take the rice off the heat and stir it up. All the water will have been absorbed into the rice. This method, if followed precisely, works for any amount of rice.

Let the rice cool and add the other ingredients, except the tomatoes and parsley. Add the vinaigrette and give the salad a few careful turns so that the vinaigrette is evenly distributed. Sprinkle the tomatoes and parsley on top and serve.

Lunch at the beach for four.

CRAB MAYONNAISE

4 paddle crabs cooked 10 minutes in boiling water
mayonnaise (see pages 20-22)
salt, pepper and lemon juice

For 2 cups of well-seasoned mayonnaise crumble the meat of 4
paddle crabs, mix it with the mayonnaise, adjust the seasoning
with salt, pepper and lemon juice and serve with raw vegetables,
boiled eggs, french bread and olives.
An excellent dip for raw vegetables and french bread.

Oysters

What can one do with fresh oysters but eat them immediately, raw? If you do find yourself with too many oysters, I recommend you invite the required number of friends, open some wine and eat the lot, raw.
Recipes for oysters bring one into the realm of fussy restaurant cooking. Remember that oysters taste like the sea, and when you tamper with this flavour it is generally lost. However, here are a few ideas.

— If you have oysters on the half shell, crumble a little blue cheese over them and slide them under a very hot grill until the cheese bubbles. Serve immediately. This works well with fresh herb butter as well. If the grill is hot, the cheese or herb butter cooks, but the oysters are only warmed. The cooked cheese and warmed oyster combination is very good.

— Let 300 ml cream come to room temperature. Empty it into a bowl and squeeze in the juice of a lemon. Set aside for 20 minutes at room temperature, then stir slowly and it will thicken. You now have a variety of clotted cream, delicious with fresh oysters, brown bread, cracked black pepper and more lemon juice.

— Fresh oysters on the half shell with tabasco and lime wedges as an hors d'oeuvre.

— Make oyster wontons by filling fresh wonton wrappers with an oyster, a little chopped ginger and spring onion, deepfry until golden and serve with soy sauce or sweet chilli sauce on the side.

OYSTERS IN PASTRY

**4 rectangles of cooked flaky pastry measuring
10 cm x 5 cm
50 g butter
2 spring onions thinly sliced
2 cos lettuce leaves thinly sliced
2 dozen raw oysters and their liquor
25 ml dry white wine
150 ml cream
juice of half a lemon
pepper and salt**

Use commercially made flaky pastry and follow the baking instructions on the packet.

Make the pastry in advance, cool and slice them through the middle horizontally.

Heat the oven to 180°C and reheat the pastries, being careful not to burn them.

In a frying pan melt the butter and add the oysters, spring onions and the lettuce and fry them gently for 1 minute.

Place $1/4$ of the oyster mixture onto each bottom half of the pastries.

Add the oyster liquor, the wine then the cream to the pan, and reduce by boiling it to the consistency of thick cream. Taste and season with lemon juice, salt and pepper. Pour the sauce over the oysters and put the pastry tops back on the top.

Serve immediately.

Serves four as a first course.

OYSTER, BACON AND SPINACH CREAM

A warming soup for cold days.

50 g butter
1 small leek finely sliced
1 small onion finely diced
1 tb parsley chopped
150 g rindless bacon cut into 2 cm dice
50 g flour
50 ml dry white wine
600 ml milk
2 dozen Pacific oysters (and their liquor) chopped roughly
half a bunch of spinach finely chopped
juice of half a lemon
1 pinch of nutmeg
salt and pepper
butter and parsley for serving

Melt the butter over a gentle heat. Add the leek, onion, parsley and bacon and fry without browning them for 5 minutes. Add the flour and stir well, then add the wine, stirring continuously. Stir in the milk. Keep stirring until it comes to the boil, then add the oysters and their liquor.

Simmer for 10 minutes on a very low heat. If the soup becomes too thick, thin it with a little more milk. Add the spinach, taste and season with the lemon juice, nutmeg and salt and pepper. Continue to simmer the soup until the spinach is soft. The soup should be thick and creamy.

Just before serving stir in a generous knob of butter and serve with more chopped parsley.

Serves four.

Paua

PAUA WITH LEMON

> **fresh paua**
> **a little flour**
> **butter**
> **lemons**
> **black pepper**

Detach the paua from the shell with a sharp knife, then take out
the soft middle part. Tenderise the remaining meat as you would a
tough steak by beating it, then slice it.

Dust the slices with flour and pan-fry them in butter, squeezing a
little lemon juice over them as they cook. Do not overcook them.
Serve immediately with lemon wedges and ground black pepper.
The soft part can be cooked the same way, but slice it after it is
cooked.

PAUA SASHIMI-STYLE

My favourite way of eating paua follows the Japanese formula for sashimi (raw fish), which ensures that the paua's paradoxical rich yet delicate flavour is best appreciated. Try them like this.

Tenderise the paua as described on page 71 and slice it thinly. Take a pair of chopsticks and eat the paua with finely chopped raw ginger, Japanese soy sauce and Japanese horseradish (wasabi). Gaze at the sea as you eat. Sublime!

Cockles, pipi and tuatua

Do not scorn these humble creatures. While they might not be the stuff of grand cuisine, they do make tasty additions to many dishes. Use them as a delicious extra on a homemade pizza. Substitute the crab in the crab salad on page 66 with any of these three. Use them as a filling for the omelette on page 62. Best of all, gather cockles, pipi and tuatua yourself and cook them on the barbecue. Take them straight off the fire (with shells discarded, naturally) and stuff between slices of fresh bread and butter with a little vinegar.

STEAMED SHELLFISH WITH OLIVE OIL AND POTATOES

1.5 kg live shellfish such as cockles, tuatua and
pipi (or mussels)
50 ml extra virgin olive oil
3 cloves garlic finely chopped
zest of 1 lemon
1/2 tsp freshly ground black pepper
1 cup Italian parsley leaves coarsely chopped
3 medium waxy potatoes peeled and cooked in
boiling water until just tender, well drained and
chopped into 3 cm dice

Put everything into a large saucepan over a high heat. Shake the pan occassionally to prevent sticking.

Lift the lid to check on progress and remove the shellfish to a warmed serving platter as they open. (Even shellfish of the same variety open at different rates, so they should be removed as they are ready to prevent overcooking which makes them tough.)

Pile everything onto the serving platter and pour on the liquid from the pan.

Serves four.

Scallops

SCALLOPS WITH PASTA AND PESTO

250 g fresh fettucine, or the equivalent of good
quality dried pasta
2 tb olive oil
50 g butter
1 onion chopped
1 clove garlic chopped finely
1 tb parsley chopped
2 dozen shelled scallops
75 ml dry white wine
150 ml cream
100 ml pesto (see page 34)
salt and pepper
juice of 1 lemon
finely grated Parmesan

Cook the pasta in plenty of boiling, salted water.

Drain it, add the olive oil and mix it so that it does not stick together and set it to one side.

In a large frying pan melt the butter, add the onion, garlic and parsley and fry gently until the onion is golden. Turn up the heat and add the scallops. Sauté them until they are white and firm, then take them out of the pan and keep them hot.

Add the wine to the pan and boil until most of the liquid has reduced. Add the cream and bring back to the boil. Add the pasta. Stir carefully so that pasta does not stick. The sauce will thicken as the pasta heats through.

When the pasta has heated, return the scallops plus any liquid that has seeped from them. Stir in the pesto and taste the sauce. Season with the salt, pepper and lemon juice.

Pour the mixture into a warm serving dish and sprinkle with plenty of finely grated Parmesan.

Serve at once. Enough for four.

SCALLOPS WITH ALMONDS AND LEMON BUTTER

100 g butter
150 g flaked almonds toasted
1 clove garlic crushed
3 spring onions finely sliced
2 dozen scallops
25 ml brandy
juice and zest of 1 lemon
1 tb parsley chopped
pepper and salt

Melt half the butter in a large frying pan. Add the almonds, garlic and spring onions and fry gently for two minutes, then add the scallops. Cook until the scallops are white and firm, then pour over the brandy. Light the pan and let the brandy burn.

When it stops burning, add the lemon juice and zest and add the parsley. By this time the scallops will be cooked enough. Sprinkle over some pepper and salt and stir in the rest of the butter.

Serve with steamed rice.

Serves four.

SCALLOPS IN BROTH WITH GLASS NOODLES

Firm, white-skinned, boned fish can be used instead of scallops; just thinly slice it first.

1 litre chicken or fish stock
3 stalks lemongrass, white bulbous ends only, crushed
2 tb ginger chopped
2 tb coriander stalks chopped
3 cloves garlic crushed
2 hot fresh chillis chopped
1 tb tamarind paste
1 tb sugar
100 g glass (also called cellophane or beanthread) noodles soaked until soft in plenty of hot water
400 g scallops halved
2 tb fish sauce
zest of 2 limes

GARNISH
1 fresh red chilli sliced finely
coriander leaves
lime wedges

Put the stock, lemon grass, ginger, chillis, tamarind and sugar into a saucepan and bring to the boil. Simmer 5 minutes, skimming off any scum as it rises.

Remove from the heat and strain the mixture, discarding the herbs and spices.

Return to the heat and add the drained noodles and simmer until the noodles are transparent, (about 1-2 minutes).

Add the scallops, lime zest and fish sauce, bring back to the boil.

Remove from the heat and serve garnished with the sliced chilli, coriander and a lime wedge on the side.

Serves four.

SHELLFISH AND CRUSTACEANS

SKEWERED SCALLOPS

For each skewer you will need the following:
6 scallops
6 small pieces of bacon
6 pieces of onion
6 pieces of red capsicum
olive oil

First thread a scallop onto the skewer then a piece of bacon, then a piece of onion, then the capsicum. Repeat this sequence until the 6 scallops are on the skewer. Make up as many skewers as you need. Brush the scallops and other ingredients with olive oil and barbecue, pan-fry or grill them until they are cooked.

Serve with fresh tomato sauce (see page 30) and french bread.

The same sauce is also excellent with scallops pan-fried with a little chopped onion in olive oil. Serve them on top of hot pasta with the sauce poured over the top.

STEAMED SCALLOPS WITH RAW TOMATO
RELISH AND RICE

RELISH
8 tomatoes peeled, cored, seeded and chopped
juice of 2 lemons
zest of 1 lemon
3 cloves garlic finely chopped
$1/_4$ cup each of basil and mint leaves ripped into
small pieces
$1/_4$ cup Italian parsley chopped
salt and freshly ground black pepper

Mix everything together, seasoning well with the salt and pepper.
Set aside.

2 cups of long grain rice steamed or boiled
20 scallops steamed over high heat until just
cooked through (do not overcook)
extra virgin olive oil

To serve, put the hot rice on a warm serving platter. Arrange the
hot scallops on top. Sprinkle the relish over the scallops. Drizzle
everything with the olive oil.
Serves four.

WARM SCALLOP AND BACON SALAD

1 small lettuce or other salad greens
2 tomatoes cut into thin wedges
1 stick of celery sliced thinly
1 spring onion chopped
1 tb parsley chopped
1 tb fresh basil torn into small pieces
juice of half a lemon
100 ml cream
25 g butter
200 g rindless bacon cut into 2 cm dice
12 scallops cut in half
freshly ground black pepper

Assemble the salad first.

Wash the lettuce or greens, dry them and put them into a large salad bowl. Sprinkle over the tomatoes, celery, spring onion and herbs.

Mix the lemon juice into the cream, which should be at room temperature, and stir slowly until the cream thickens. This is the salad dressing. Put to one side.

Heat a frying pan and melt the butter. When it is hot, throw in the bacon and the scallops and pan-fry them until the scallops are just cooked and the bacon is beginning to crisp. Lift out the hot scallops and bacon with a slotted spoon and sprinkle them over the salad. Pour over the clotted cream and give the salad a couple of turns to mix it.

Grind a little black pepper over the salad, sprinkle on some more chopped parsley and serve.

Serves four.

Octopus and squid

These are a true delicacy. The squid available in fish shops has usually been frozen. While it may not be as tasty as fresh squid, the frozen variety still makes extremely good eating. It is conveniently available as 'squid tubes', which are the bodies with the head, tentacles and guts removed. However, if you should ever be lucky enough to find (or catch) whole squid, they are easy to clean and cook.

CLEANING SQUID

Pull the head and tentacles away from the body. (Save the tentacles if they are small: they are excellent quickly fried in olive oil with garlic and lemon.) Pull out the guts and feel around for the transparent internal shell and discard this, too. Scrape off the purplish skin. Rinse the body under cold water.

FRIED SQUID RINGS

squid rings
flour
olive oil
lemon wedges

Simply slice the body or tube into rings $1/2$ cm thick. Dust them in flour and fry them in hot olive oil until golden brown. Serve well drained with lemon wedges. They will not be tough if you cook them quickly, and they should have the texture of pasta cooked al dente — with just a slight resistance when bitten into.

STIRFRIED SQUID SALAD WITH
TAMARIND DRESSING

**2 squid tubes, opened flat, cut into 5 cm square
pieces
3 cloves garlic, finely chopped
1 tb ginger, finely chopped
1 tsp cracked black pepper
50 ml sesame oil
3 tb soy sauce**

Mix everything and marinate 20 minutes.

**4 tb soy oil
1 fresh chilli seeded and sliced
100 g green beans, stalk end cut off
2 cups broccoli florets
2 spring onions cut into 5 cm lengths
$1/_2$ cucumber seeded and sliced 2 cm thick
2 tomatoes cored and cut into wedges
2 tb toasted sesame seeds**

Blanch the beans and broccoli for 2 minutes in boiling water,
refresh in cold water and drain well.

**DRESSING
100 ml lime juice
2 tb palm sugar grated (or brown sugar if palm
unavailable)
2 tb tamarind concentrate
4 tb soy bean oil**

Mix everything well until the sugar has dissolved and set aside.

Heat a wok over high heat until very hot. Add the drained squid and sear all over until the squid is just cooked through. Remove and set aside.

Heat the wok again add the 4 tb soy oil and let it get hot. Add everything except the squid, tomatoes and sesame seeds. Stirfry until hot. Add the squid and tomatoes and stirfry until they are hot. Pile everything onto a serving dish and drizzle over the well-mixed dressing.

Serve immediately with rice.

Serves four to six.

OCTOPUS VINAIGRETTE

1 large octopus
150 ml olive oil
juice of a lemon
25 ml wine vinegar
2 cloves garlic crushed
salt and pepper
tomato wedges
black olives
spring onions chopped
capers
parsley chopped

Remove the head and guts of the octopus as described for squid on page 81.

Bring a large pot of salted water to the boil and simmer the octopus until tender but not disintegrating; this could take up to 1 hour and the octopus will shrink by about half. Drain and cool enough to handle then rub off any suckers and skin. Cut the octopus into bite-sized pieces.

Make a vinaigrette from the olive oil, lemon juice, wine vinegar, garlic and salt and pepper. Make sure it is well mixed.

Put the pieces of octopus into a bowl, pour over the vinaigrette and leave to stand for half an hour.

Add plenty of tomato wedges, black olives, chopped spring onions, capers and chopped parsley and toss.

Serves four.

OCTOPUS SALAD

**2 large octopus, prepared as described in the
recipe for octopus vinaigrette. Chop the tentacles
into bite-sized lengths and toss lightly in olive oil.
4 spring onions sliced
1 cucumber seeded and chopped
3 tomatoes chopped
3 cloves garlic finely chopped
1 cos lettuce finely chopped
$^1/_2$ cup each of mint, coriander and
Italian parsley, chopped
salt and pepper
juice of 2 lemons
olive oil**

**SPICE MIX
1 tb sumac (a lemony Middle Eastern herb, available from Middle Eastern or Indian shops)
$1^1/_2$ tsp sea salt
2 tb toasted sesame seeds**

Mix the spice mix together and set aside.

Mix all the salad ingredients together well, seasoning well with
salt and pepper, and drizzling liberally with the olive oil.
Heat a frying pan or the barbecue plate until very hot and sear the
octopus all over until hot and browned. Toss the hot octopus in the
spice mix until well coated.
Put the salad and octopus onto a large serving platter, give it a
brief toss and serve.
Serves six to eight.

Kina

Kina, like oysters and paua, have that unmistakable 'essence of the sea' flavour — salty with a hint of iodine. They are daunting to look at and painful to stand on, but if you like oysters and paua you will like eating the orange corals from a fresh kina. You will not enjoy it if it is not absolutely fresh.

The best way to eat kina is straight from the sea, cut in half, rinsed in sea water, with lemon and fresh bread.

Provided they are fresh, a few corals make a delicious addition to fresh mayonnaise (see page 22) or sauce hollandaise (see page 26). Crush the corals with a fork and stir them into the sauce at the last minute. They transform any dish from the delicious to the exceptional. A few corals sprinkled over seafood soups or fish stews have the same effect.

Freshwater
fish

Salmon, trout and salmon trout

The following recipes are interchangeable for salmon, trout and salmon trout as the three species are similar in flavour and texture and suit the same cooking methods. Salmon trout is not, by the way, a strange mutation resulting from the mis-alliance of a trout and a salmon, but a distinct species of fish considered in Europe to be the finest of the three.

Here are three quick 'carpaccio' using raw salmon which make excellent first courses or light lunches.

SALMON CARPACCIO WITH WATERMELON AND ROCKET

**500 g salmon fillet, boned, sliced obliquely
towards the tail end, in paper-thin slices
extra virgin olive oil
cracked black pepper and sea salt
150 g rocket leaves
1 cup cherry tomatoes halved
1^1/$_2$ cups watermelon seeded and peeled
juice of ^{1}/$_2$ lemon**

Lie the salmon out flat on a large tray and drizzle it with a little extra virgin olive oil and sprinkle it with the pepper and salt. Set aside for 10 minutes.

Arrange the rocket and cherry tomatoes on a large flat platter. Lie the salmon slices on top.

Purée the watermelon and lemon juice until frothy and pour it all over the salmon.

Serve immediately.

Serves four.

SALMON CARPACCIO WITH LIME AND GINGER

**500 g salmon fillet boned and sliced obliquely
towards the tail end in paper-thin slices
$1/2$ cup extra virgin olive oil
2 tb ginger cut into very thin matchsticks
zest of 2 limes
1 fresh hot chilli seeded and sliced finely
(optional)
$1/2$ cup coriander leaves
freshly ground black pepper
sea salt
2 limes halved**

Lie the salmon out flat on a large platter. Sprinkle the ginger, lime zest, chilli and coriander leaves over the salmon. Season well with the salt and pepper. Drizzle the oil over everything.

Set aside covered for 1 hour.

Serve with the lime halves on the side for squeezing over the salmon before eating.

Serves four.

SALMON CARPACCIO WITH DRIED TOMATOES AND OLIVES

**500 g salmon fillet, boned and sliced obliquely
towards the tail end in paper-thin slices
100 g rocket leaves
sea salt and black pepper
1/2 cup sundried tomatoes drained and sliced
thinly
1/2 cup green olives
extra virgin olive oil
2 lemons halved**

Lie the salmon slices out flat on a large platter. Put the rocket leaves in a heap in the middle of the salmon. Season with pepper and salt. Sprinkle the tomatoes and olives over the salmon and rocket.
Drizzle extra virgin olive oil over everything.
Serve the lemon halves on the side to be squeezed over the salad before eating.
Serves four.

HOME-CURED SALMON, A VARIATION OF SWEDISH GRAVLAX

Curing salmon is easy and well worth the effort. It can be used instead of commercially smoked salmon in most situations and has a more interesting texture and flavour.

**700 g salmon fillet, skin on but boned, cut into 2 equal pieces
1¹/2 tb Maldon sea salt
1 tb brown sugar
2 tb brandy or better still Russian vodka
4 tb dill chopped
1 tsp cracked black pepper
zest of 1 lemon**

Mix the sugar, salt and alcohol to a thick paste.

Put one of the salmon pieces, skin side down, into a nonreactive shallow dish just big enough to hold it.

Spread the paste onto the flesh of the salmon in the dish. Sprinkle the dill, pepper and zest over the paste. Lie the other piece of salmon on top, flesh side down, so that you have a sandwich. Cover with foil and put some weights on top (a couple of 400 gm unopened cans of something usually works).

Leave in the refrigerator 24 hours or up to 5 days but turn once every day.

Serve thinly sliced, discarding the skin, as an hors d'oeuvre with brown bread, sour cream and wholegrain mustard or in bagels with cream cheese.

Serves four to six.

HOME-SMOKED SALMON

Hot-smoking salmon in a fish smoker on the barbecue or stove results in a completely different product from commercial cold-smoked salmon and I prefer its robust taste.

**1 kg side salmon, boned, left whole or cut into slices
6 tb brown sugar
1/2 tsp Maldon sea salt
extra virgin olive oil**

Mix the sugar and salt with enough of the olive oil to make a thick spreadable paste. Spread this over the flesh side of the salmon and set aside 30 minutes.

Put 2 handfuls of untreated wood chips into a small fish smoker.

Put the salmon on the smoking rack, skin side down, and place inside the smoker. Put the lid on and put the smoker over high heat until wisps of smoke appear from under the lid. Turn the heat down to moderate and smoke 15 minutes until the salmon is just cooked through; do not overcook.

Remove from the smoker, invert the rack onto a flat tray if the fillet is whole, and cool the salmon slightly.

Peel off the skin. Re-invert for serving. Serve warm or cold.

For a more fragrant taste substitute the wood chips for the following smoking mix which is based on a recipe by Christine Manfield, the chef of Sydney's Paramount Restaurant.

**1 1/2 cups oolong tea leaves
zest of 1 orange
4 tb jasmine rice
2 tb brown sugar
2 dried bay leaves crumbled**

Mix well before using. Will keep for up to a month in an airtight container.

IDEAS FOR HOME-SMOKED SALMON:

— serve with toasted brioche and crème fraiche

— serve with oven-roasted tomatoes and rocket leaves

— serve with latkes, the little grated potato fritters of Jewish cookery

— make a vegetable risotto based on fish or chicken stock and serve with the home-smoked salmon flaked on top

— serve with finely sliced red onion inside an omelette

— make club sandwiches with home-smoked salmon, cream cheese and thinly sliced cucumber for a deluxe afternoon tea or with drinks

SMOKED SALMON WITH BLINIS AND CLOTTED CREAM

Blinis are the little Russian yeast pancakes that are often served warm with smoked salmon. The following recipe for blinis is enough for six.

600 ml milk
2 tsp dried yeast
pinch of sugar
225 g plain white flour
225 g buckwheat flour
pinch of salt
250 g melted butter
2 eggs separated

Warm the milk to blood heat. Take 50 ml of the milk and mix in the yeast and the sugar. Set it aside until the yeast begins to work.

Put both types of flour and the salt into a large, warmed bowl and make a well in the middle. Pour in the remaining milk and beat until smooth. Add the yeast and mix thoroughly. Cover with a damp cloth and leave in a warm place to rise. When doubled in bulk add the melted butter and the egg yolks. Mix thoroughly. Beat the egg whites until stiff and fold them into the mixture. Cover with a damp cloth and leave in a warm place to double in bulk again.

Heat a large frying pan until it is very hot. Wipe the surface of the pan with a kitchen towel dipped in melted butter. Drop small spoonfuls of the mixture into the pan. The blinis should have a diameter of no more than 6 cm. When bubbles appear in the upper surface of the blini, they are ready to be turned over. Cook on both sides until they are golden brown.

Serve the warm blinis with thin slices of smoked salmon (commercial or home), clotted cream (that is, cream thickened by adding a little lemon juice and stirring slowly) and slices of cucumber.

A few nips of Russian vodka, well chilled, go down very well with this dish.

WHOLE BAKED SALMON OR TROUT

*Few of us have rectangular fish kettles large enough to accom-
modate even a moderately sized fish, so tin foil is the answer
for this type of fish cookery.*

1 large whole salmon or trout
150 ml dry white wine
parsley
2 bay leaves
2 cloves
strip of lemon peel with pith removed
half a small onion finely sliced
salt and black pepper
butter

Weigh the fish.

Tear off a piece of tin foil larger than the fish and sit it in a baking
dish. Put the cleaned salmon or trout on top and pour over enough
water to make a 1 cm deep pool. Pour over the dry white wine. Put
in a few sprigs of parsley, the bay leaves, cloves, lemon peel and
onion. Sprinkle with a little salt and black pepper and dot with
small pieces of butter.

Pull up the sides of the tin foil until they meet and twist them
together so that you have a sealed parcel that is not tight against
the fish.

Bake at 150°C for 1 hour for the first 2 kg and 10 minutes for each
500 g after that. When it is cooked, drain off the liquid and discard.
Carefully slide the fish onto a serving dish. If you wish, expose the
pink flesh by gently scraping the skin off with a knife.

Serve with hollandaise sauce (see page 26) if you are serving it
hot or a herbed mayonnaise (see pages 20-22) if you are serving
it cold.

Whether hot or cold, serve the fish with small, whole new potatoes, plainly boiled and tossed in parsley butter.

Serves four.

SALMON IN SWEET SOY SAUCE WITH PICKLED CUCUMBER AND NOODLES

The marinade is from Madhur Jaffrey's excellent Far Eastern Cookery *(BBC Books 1989) and is a traditional Japanese marinade which I've found indispensable. Good as a marinade for most sorts of fish and seafood.*

700g salmon fillet, skinned, boned and cut into 4 slices

MARINADE
150 ml Japanese soy sauce
150 ml sake
6 tb sugar
Put everything into a small saucepan and bring to the boil, stirring to dissolve the sugar. Boil a few minutes and remove from the heat and cool completely.

Put the salmon into a small flat dish and pour over 200 ml of the marinade. Marinate 1 hour, turning frequently.

Drain, skewer the length of each salmon slice crosswise with 2 soaked bamboo skewers.

Grill or barbecue over moderate heat so the salmon is just cooked but starting to brown. Serve with:

— plenty of freshly cooked Japanese noodles that have a little sesame oil stirred through them.

— the remaining 100 ml marinade as a dipping sauce.

— some pink Japanese pickled ginger.

— $^1/_2$ a cucumber sliced paper-thin which has been sprinkled with salt for 30 minutes, washed well in cold water, squeezed dry and dressed with the following:

$^1/_4$ cup rice vinegar, 4 tb water, $^1/_2$ tsp salt, 1 tsp sugar mixed well to dissolve the sugar and salt. Serves four.

97

SALMON STEAKS OR FILLETS WITH CUCUMBER AND CAPERS

Whenever I cook this dish I am always amazed by the delicious flavour the cucumbers give the sauce.

50 g butter
1 tb onion or, preferably, shallot chopped
4 steaks or small fillets of salmon per person
flour for dusting fish
1 tb chives chopped
1 tb capers drained
half a telegraph cucumber sliced thinly
50 ml dry vermouth
200 ml cream
salt and pepper
juice of half a lemon

Preheat the oven to 200°C.
In a large ovenproof frying pan melt the butter over a gentle heat. Do not let it burn. Add the onion and cook it gently for 1 minute. Flour the fish and place it in the pan. Cook 1 minute on each side but do not brown it. Add the chives, capers and cucumber. Pour in the vermouth and bring to the boil. Add the cream and boil again. As soon as the cream boils, take the pan from the heat and put it in the hot oven for 15 minutes. By this time a fork will go into the fish and come out cleanly.
Carefully remove the salmon and put it onto a warm serving dish. Keep it warm. Put the frying pan onto a fast heat and reduce the sauce until it is the consistency of thick cream.
Taste and season with the salt, pepper and lemon juice.
Serves four.

STEAMED SALMON WITH MLLE LE CLERC'S OLIVE OIL AND PARSLEY DRESSING

800 g salmon fillet, skinned, boned and sliced into
4 pieces, steamed over moderate heat until just
cooked through and served with:

DRESSING
$1^1/_2$ cups Italian parsley leaves
$^1/_2$ cup capers
1 cup extra virgin olive oil
freshly ground black pepper
Put everything into the food processer and
process to a smooth purée. This dressing is also
good with steamed scallops, crayfish or firm
white fish.

SALMON WITH SORREL

50 g butter
4 fresh salmon steaks about 150-200 g each
flour for dusting
50 ml dry white wine
300 g sorrel leaves washed and roughly chopped
200 ml cream
1 egg yolk
salt and pepper
juice of half a lemon
1 tb parsley chopped

In a frying pan melt the butter.

Flour the fish and pan-fry it gently on each side. Let it brown just a little. When it is almost cooked through, take it out of the pan and put it on a serving dish then into a hot oven. It will finish cooking as you make the sauce.

Put the pan back over a high heat and add the wine and sorrel. Bring it to the boil and scrape the pan with a wooden spoon to dislodge any pieces of fish adhering to the pan. Add 150 ml of the cream and bring to the boil.

Meanwhile, beat the egg yolk with the remaining 50 ml of cream. When the sauce has reduced, take the pan off the heat and whisk in the egg yolk mixture. The yolk and cream mix will thicken and enrich the sauce. Do not put the sauce back on the heat as it will curdle.

Take the dish with the fish on it out of the oven and pour any liquid that has seeped from the fish into the sauce. Stir it in, taste the sauce and season it with the salt, pepper and lemon juice.

Pour the sauce over the fish and serve with chopped parsley.

Enough for four.

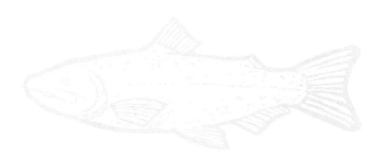

LEFTOVERS

If you have some leftover poached salmon, trout or salmon trout flake the flesh, sprinkle it with lemon juice and chopped fresh dill and put it inside a runny omelette at the last minute.

Another way of using leftover salmon is in a cucumber salad, as follows. Peel and slice very thinly a whole telegraph cucumber. Sprinkle it with a little salt and let it sit for half an hour in a china bowl. Rinse all the salt off under running water and squeeze it dry. Put a few leaves of your preferred salad greens in a shallow bowl. Mix 100 ml of cream with the juice of half a lemon until the cream thickens. Mix the cream, cucumber slices and the leftover fish and arrange on top of the salad greens. Sprinkle with pepper, salt and chopped parsley and fresh dill. Serve with french bread.

TROUT WITH NUTS

A variation of the old trout almondine recipe.

25 ml olive oil
150 g chopped nuts (use any nuts except peanuts
or walnuts)
4 trout steaks 2.5 cm thick
1 small onion chopped
8 tb red wine vinegar
1 tb capers drained
chopped parsley

Preheat the oven to 200°C. Heat the olive oil in a heavy frying pan. Press the chopped nuts into each side of the trout steaks and put the steaks into the oil. Sprinkle any excess nuts over the fish. Fry the fish gently on each side until the steaks are just starting to brown. Throw in the chopped onion and put 2 tb of vinegar over each steak. Put the pan in the oven and let the fish cook through. When the fish is cooked, remove to a serving dish and keep it hot. Put the pan back onto a gentle heat and add the capers. When the capers are heated through, pour the mixture over the fish.
Sprinkle with plenty of chopped parsley and serve.
Serves four.

TERRINE OF TROUT WITH POTATOES AND CREAM

75 g butter
1 onion thinly sliced
1/2 stick of celery finely sliced
1 clove garlic finely chopped
100 ml dry white wine
1 tsp green peppercorns
1/2 tsp salt
3 waxy potatoes peeled and boiled until cooked but not disintegrating
1 kg skinned, boned trout fillets
2 eggs beaten
300 ml cream
2 tb parsley chopped

Heat the oven to 200°C.

Choose a large, heavy, ovenproof casserole for this dish, preferably with a lid, but tin foil can be used. Melt the butter in the casserole over a gentle heat and add the onion, celery and garlic. Gently fry until the onion is golden but not brown. Add the wine and continue cooking until half the wine has disappeared. Add the peppercorns and salt. Stir the mixture well.

Turn off the heat, slice half the potatoes and put them on top of the onion mixture.

Next put in the trout so that you have a layer of trout and slice the other half of the potatoes on top.

Mix the beaten eggs with the cream and parsley and pour this over the other ingredients. Push down the potatoes and fish so that the liquid can be seen.

Put the lid or tin foil on the casserole and bake it in the oven for 40 to 45 minutes or until the terrine has set firmly.

Serve with plainly cooked green vegetables.

Serves six.

Whitebait

Like crayfish, fresh New Zealand whitebait is so expensive and so delicious that one is thankful to cook and eat it in the simplest way possible. After experimenting with it extensively I always seem return to fritters and their variations. Here are two.

DAVID'S WHITEBAIT FRITTER
As cooked at the French Cafe in Auckland

FOR ONE SERVING:
2 eggs
3 tb South Island whitebait
$1/2$ tsp baking powder
1 tsp spring onion finely chopped
parsley chopped
black pepper and salt
50 ml ghee or clarified butter

Preheat the oven to 200°C.

Into a bowl break the eggs, add the whitebait, baking powder, spring onion, chopped parsley, black pepper and salt. Beat everything with a fork until it is amalgamated.

Heat a 15 cm frying pan. Add the ghee or clarified butter and let it get very hot.

Pour in the whitebait mixture and stir it until you see the mixture catch on the bottom of the pan. Take the pan off the heat and put it into a hot oven until the fritter puffs up. Remove the pan from the oven and flip the fritter. (David would throw it into the air with a look of supreme concentration.) Cook it for 30 seconds and flip it again.

Serve on a warm plate with freshly cut lemon wedges.

WHITEBAIT FRITTERS WITH ASIAN HERBS

2 eggs separated
500 g whitebait
1 tb coriander leaves and stalks finely chopped
1 small hot green chilli
1 tb lemongrass, tender inside of the bulbous end
only, finely chopped
2 tb Chinese chives chopped
1 tb fish sauce
vegetable oil for frying

Beat the egg whites until stiff.

Beat the yolks and mix them with everything else. Fold the beaten whites into the mixture.

Fry dessertspoonfuls in hot vegetable oil on each side until golden.

Drain on paper towels.

Serve with the Vietnamese dipping sauce, Nuoc Cham, on page 32.

Makes about 24.

Eel

Try to get your eel live and kill it by whacking it on the back of the head. Then skin it by pouring boiling water over it, then nicking the skin around the head and peeling off the skin. Do not bother boning it as this takes considerable skill and the flesh falls off the bones anyway if it is well cooked. Cut the eel into manageable lengths, about 10 cm, and it is ready to cook.

BARBECUED EEL WITH MUSTARD

eel pieces
1/2 cup good French mustard
50 ml dry white wine
25 ml olive oil

Mix the mustard with the dry white wine and olive oil. Pour this over the eel pieces and marinate for 2 hours. Take the eel out of the marinade, shake off any excess mustard mixture and barbecue over a slow fire, or under a grill until the meat can be lifted away from the backbone easily. As they are cooking, brush the eel pieces with any extra marinade.

BAKED EEL WITH HERB BUTTER

eel pieces
fresh herb butter (see pages 23-25)
white wine or cider

Set the oven at 200˚C. Put the pieces of eel into a roasting dish and dot them with pieces of herb butter. Sprinkle over a little white wine or cider and bake until the eel comes away from the bone. Serve with lemon wedges and french bread.

FRESHWATER FISH

SMOKED EEL

Smoked eel is another delicacy that needs an accompaniment
of only brown bread and butter and lemon juice.
However, the following salad is a good variation.

250 g smoked eel fillets
100 g roasted almonds roughly chopped
3 sticks celery sliced thinly
2 oranges (cut the skins off with a sharp knife so
that no pith remains, cut around the core and
slice the flesh)
1 spring onion finely chopped
10 young spinach leaves washed and torn into
bite-sized pieces
100 ml cream
juice of half a lemon
pepper and salt

Cut the eel into long, thin strips. Put all the ingredients except the cream and lemon juice and seasonings into a salad bowl.

Mix the cream with lemon juice and season it with the pepper and salt. Pour the cream mixture over the salad.

Give it a few turns and serve with fresh wholemeal bread and butter.

Serves four as an entrée.

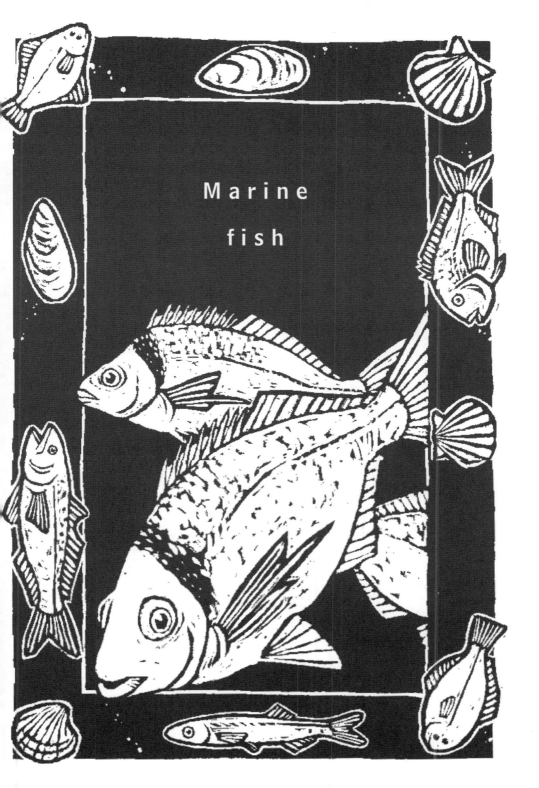

Marine

fish

White fish

NEW ZEALAND FISH STEW

The appeal of bouillabaisse (perhaps the most famous fish stew of all) seems to lie in its reputation for being 'real' French food, and its high proportion of seafood. However, bouillabaisse is a regional dish. It can be made only on the Mediterranean coast of France as it depends on varieties of fish found only in the waters off that coast. Bouillabaisse made elsewhere will never taste like the one made in Marseilles.

Don't bother to try to reproduce it. It is the method by which it is made that is important. Bouillabaisse is fish and shellfish, combined with aromatic vegetables and herbs, wine, olive oil and saffron, quickly and furiously boiled in water. The result is two dishes to be served together: a delicious, fresh-tasting soup and an aromatic platter of fish and seafood. Using this method you can make your own regional version of bouillabaisse. Such a stew made in Auckland will be different from one made in Christchurch, and it will probably be different each time you make it because of variations in the ingredients available.

100 ml olive oil
1 onion chopped
4 tomatoes chopped
4 cloves of garlic chopped
1 tb fennel leaves chopped
1 bay leaf
pinch of saffron
2 kg assorted fish (anything will do, except the
oily varieties) gutted, scaled and cut into slices
150 ml dry white wine
1 or 2 dozen live shellfish (mussels, pipi, cockles,
scallops)
a crayfish, if you have one, cut down the middle
4 large crabs halved and washed
1 squid cleaned and sliced
any other seafood that takes your fancy
parsley for garnishing, chopped

Put the oil, vegetables and herbs into a large pot. Add the thicker pieces of fish, which will need longer cooking, and the wine. Cover with boiling water. Put the pot over a fierce heat and boil rapidly for 4 minutes, then add the remaining fish and shellfish and bring to the boil. Boil for a further 5 minutes. Carefully take out the fish and shellfish and arrange them in a serving dish. Everything will have cooked and the shellfish will have opened.

Bring the liquid in the pot to the boil, taste it and season it. Strain it into a separate dish.

Sprinkle chopped parsley over both dishes and serve them with bread and/or potatoes, a bowl of grated gruyère cheese, and a bowl of aïoli or rouille (see pages 21 and 35).

Enough for ten people.

LA BOURRIDE

Bourride and bouillabaisse are the two famous fish soup/stews from the south of France. Snapper, John Dory, hapuku, bluenose, orange roughy, tarakihi or gurnard are all excellent cooked this way.

Bourride is fish poached in a fish stock which is thickened at the last moment by whisking in garlic mayonnaise. The result is moist fillets of fish in a pale yellow, creamy garlic soup. It requires boned fillets of fish, thereby avoiding the shells and bones that can make eating bouillabaisse tedious. Some cooks add peeled tomatoes to the fish while it is poaching, but this is a matter of taste. Bourride is always served with plainly cooked potatoes, making it a filling, comforting dish. The only prerequisite is a liking for garlic.

First, make a garlic mayonnaise (see page 21). When the mayonnaise is complete, stir into it 3 extra egg yolks and mix them in well. The extra yolks ensure that the mayonnaise will be an effective 'liaison' or thickening agent. Set the mayonnaise to one side.

olive oil
3 or 4 tomatoes cored, peeled, seeded and chopped
the white of a leek finely sliced
1 clove garlic crushed
3 or 4 medium-sized fillets of white fish boned
500 ml fish stock
1 large sprig fresh thyme

MARINE FISH

Put a little olive oil in a deep frying pan and let it heat.

Add the tomatoes, the leek and the garlic then add the fish. Cover with the stock and add the sprig of thyme. Simmer the fish until it is just cooked. Remove the fish from the liquid and keep the fish hot. Discard the thyme sprig.

Boil the liquid then take it off the heat. Working quickly, drop a large spoonful of garlic mayonnaise into the hot liquid and whisk it until it has dissolved and amalgamated with the liquid.

If the sauce seems too thin, repeat the process with more mayonnaise.

If it is too thick, thin it with a little cream or extra stock.

If the sauce cools down, you can very carefully warm it over a gentle heat. However, if it even approaches boiling point it will curdle, so be careful. If it does curdle, put it into the food processor and whisk it on the highest speed to make it creamy again and carefully reheat.

Pour the sauce over the fish and serve with potatoes and a sprinkle of chopped parsley.

Enough for four people.

SOUTH INDIAN FISH AND VEGETABLE CURRY

SPICE MIX
100 ml coconut cream
50 g desiccated coconut
4 green chillis chopped
2 cups coriander leaves
juice and zest of 2-3 limes
3 cloves garlic chopped
$1/_2$ tsp ground turmeric
2 tb cumin seeds toasted
$1/_2$ tsp salt

Process everything in the food processor to a thick cream and set aside.

500 g firm white fish fillets, skinned, boned and
thickly sliced
2 medium potatoes peeled and cut into 3 cm dice
1 cup pumpkin after it has been peeled, seeded
and cut into 3 cm dice
10 spinach leaves
150 ml plain unsweetened yoghurt

Put the potatoes and pumpkin into a small saucepan and just cover with water. Bring to the boil and cook until the vegetables are tender but not mushy. Add the spice mix and mix well. Simmer 5 minutes. Add the spinach, fish and yoghurt. Mix carefully. Bring back to the boil.

Taste and season.

Put in a serving bowl and serve with rice.

Serves four.

FISH BROTH WITH FETTUCINE

2 litres fish stock
250 g fish — snapper, tarakihi, gurnard, hapuku or
John Dory are all suitable, boned and filleted
250 g fresh fettucine (or the same weight of dried
pasta, but you will need to cook it first)
6 tomatoes cored, peeled, seeded and chopped
1 tb chives chopped
1 tb parsley chopped
1 clove garlic finely chopped
100 ml dry white wine
1 tb olive oil
$1/_2$ tsp sugar
salt and black pepper for seasoning
finely grated Parmesan

Boil the stock until it has reduced in volume by one quarter.

Dice the fish into 2 cm cubes and set aside.

When the stock has reduced, add the fettucine and all other ingredients except the fish and cheese. Simmer until the pasta is
cooked. (If you are using precooked pasta, just add it to the stock
and proceed with the recipe.) Take the soup off the heat and add
the diced fish. The fish will cook in the hot soup. Taste and season
with salt and black pepper.

Serve with Parmesan and more chopped chives sprinkled on top.

The fish can be substituted for scallops or crayfish for a grander
soup.

Serves four.

MARINE FISH

FRIED FISH FILLETS

Fresh fish fillets fried crisp in olive oil are a true delight.

Dust fillets of fish in flour seasoned with salt and freshly ground black pepper. Heat a heavy frying pan and pour in a little olive oil. Heat the oil until it is hot but not smoking and carefully place the fish in it. Turn the heat up to full to compensate for the heat lost when the fish goes in. Fry the fish on each side until it is crisp and golden.

If the fillets are unusually thick, turn the heat down a little once the oil has regained its heat, or the fish will burn before it is cooked through.

When it is cooked, drain it well on a paper towel and serve with one of the sauces and accompaniments on pages 19-35.

FRIED, GRILLED OR BARBECUED SMALL FISH

Small fish cooked this way may sound unremarkable but handled properly, with due regard for the temperament of the ingredients, meals of fish cooked this way, will be enthusiastically received, the highest compliment for any cook.

Use the freshest fish, the best olive oil you can find and cook the fish carefully.

Small fish such as anchovies, sardines (the adult of the species being called pilchards or herrings), piper (also called garfish), small yellow-eyed mullet (often wrongly called herrings) and the miscellaneous 'sprats' which are caught by children off wharves, all make good eating.

Gut but do not scale before cooking.

Panfrying whole in very hot olive oil for immediate consumption is the fastest and arguably the most delicious way of dealing with an assortment of these fish.

They can also be lightly dusted in seasoned flour or polenta before frying or beheaded, slit down the belly, opened out flat, have the backbone carefully removed and be dipped in flour and beaten egg and be fried like a big fritter.

These fish are also good grilled or barbecued as are small fish too large to fit in a frying pan but too small to feed more than one person (eg small gurnard, snapper, flounder, leatherjacket or seaperch).

Gut and scale these fish before cooking. Make a few diagonal slashes on each side of the fish.

Grilling or barbecuing is the quintessential Mediterranean method for cooking fresh fish. Healthy and simple, it can be used for a special dinner party or for an unpretentious family meal.

Make sure the grill or barbecue is preheated, or the charcoal barbecue has a good bed of embers before attempting to cook. Oil the grill and the fish and baste them with olive oil as they cook.

117

Plainly grilled or barbecued small fish hardly need anything except fresh lemon, sea salt and black pepper to accompany them, but check the preceding section on sauces and accompaniments for suitable additions.

Other ideas include:
— fresh herbs stuffed inside the fish before cooking.
— balsamic vinegar (not necessarily the oldest, most expensive you can buy) or sherry vinegar, sprinkled on the fish after it has been cooked.
— mashed floury potatoes well seasoned with pepper, salt, garlic and parsley.
— creamed spinach.
— vegetables sliced thinly and grilled or barbecued with olive oil, garlic, salt and pepper.
— roasted red or yellow capsicums, peeled, seeded and sliced and mixed with a little olive oil, capers, and balsamic vinegar.
— plain, unsweetened, natural yoghurt flavoured with salt, pepper, crushed garlic and toasted sesame seeds.
— sumac, a lemony Middle Eastern herb, sprinkled over the fish after cooking.

SPRATS OR YELLOW-EYED MULLET WITH BASIL AND GARLIC

Gut the fish and inside each one put a few basil leaves and a piece of garlic. Dust the fish well with wholemeal flour. Heat enough olive oil in a large heavy frying pan until it is very hot. Carefully put the fish into the hot oil and fry quickly on both sides until they are crisp and golden. Serve immediately with plenty of lemon wedges.

2 fresh sprats or yellow-eyed mullet per person
fresh basil leaves
garlic
wholemeal flour for dusting fish
olive oil
lemon wedges

PENNE WITH OLIVE OIL AND FISH CRUMBS

**400 g penne pasta cooked al dente in plenty of boiling
salted water
4 large whole bulbs of garlic rubbed with olive oil and
roasted at 180°C for 1 hour until tender and melting.
Detach the cloves and peel them.
250 g firm white fish fillets, skinned and boned,
cut into 2 cm dice
2 tb fresh marjoram or oregano leaves
zest of 1 lemon
salt and pepper
100 ml plus 4 tb olive oil**

While the pasta is cooking, heat the 4 tb oil in a frying pan until hot but not smoking.

Add fish and fry until crisp and golden. Scrape up the crispy bits with a wooden spoon as it fries.

Drain the hot pasta and put in a warmed bowl.

Add the fish and all the other ingredients, and mix well.

Season well with salt and pepper.

Serve with extra olive oil for drizzling.

Serves four.

SNAPPER WITH TOFU, GREENS AND NOODLES

1.5 litres fish or chicken stock
300 g tofu cut into 3 cm dice
400 g skinned, boned snapper fillets cut
into large bite-size pieces
200 g thick egg noodles, cooked al dente in plenty
of boiling water
1 cm x 2 cm piece peeled ginger sliced paper-thin
zest of 1 lemon
2 cloves garlic sliced paper-thin
3 spring onions sliced diagonally
1 baby bok choy, leaves detached from the base
3 cups watercress sprigs
10 dried Chinese mushrooms soaked 20 minutes
in hot water, drained, stalks discarded, sliced
thinly

Bring stock to the boil. Add the ginger, zest, garlic, noodles, tofu, bok choy, mushrooms and spring onions. Bring back to the boil, add the snapper and watercress, remove from the heat (the heat of the soup will cook the fish), and serve in large bowls with chopsticks, spoons and a small side dish of light soy sauce that has some finely sliced green chilli in it as a dipping sauce.
Serves four.

SNAPPER WITH GREEN HERBS

200 g butter
flour for dusting fish
4 medium-sized snapper fillets skinned and boned
1 cup chopped mixed green herbs (sorrel should predomi-
nate; do not use rosemary or sage)
1 clove garlic finely chopped
zest of 1 lemon
50 ml dry white wine
salt and pepper

Melt half the butter in a large frying pan.

Flour the fish and fry it gently until it is golden and cooked through. Sprinkle over the herbs, the lemon zest and add the wine. Add the remaining butter cut into cubes. Season with salt and pepper and turn up the heat.

The butter and wine will amalgamate quickly into a syrupy sauce and the flavour of the herbs will permeate the fish. Serve immediately with french bread.

Serves four.

MARINE FISH

PIERRE'S SNAPPER WITH SCALLOPS AND LOVAGE

Lovage is a leafy herb with a flavour like young celery. If you do not have lovage, use the inside pale leaves from a bunch of celery.

4 medium-sized snapper fillets skinned and boned
100 g butter
1 shallot chopped
100 ml dry white wine
1 dozen scallops sliced
1 handful of lovage or young celery leaves
1 tsp parsley chopped
150 ml cream
pepper and salt
lemon juice

Pan-fry the snapper fillets in the butter until they are almost cooked, then put them on a serving dish and keep them hot. Add the shallot. Fry it gently for 1 minute then add the wine. Stir with a wooden spoon to pick up any pieces of shallot or fish adhering to the pan.

Boil the wine and the shallot until it is reduced by half, then add the sliced scallops, lovage and parsley. Add the cream and bring to the boil. Take out the scallops and arrange them over the fish. Boil the sauce until it is the consistency of thick cream. Pour in any liquid that has seeped from the fish and the scallops.

Taste the sauce and season with salt, pepper and lemon juice. Pour the sauce over the fish and sprinkle with more chopped parsley.

Serves four.

BABY RED SNAPPER BAKED WITH LEEKS AND TOMATOES

These jewel-like fish are often available in fish shops and are worth looking for. The flesh is superb and they are inexpensive. Allow one per person if you can get small ones, as a platter of baby red snapper looks impressive.

50 ml olive oil
1 onion chopped
2 leeks sliced
2 tb fresh coriander chopped
1 tb parsley chopped
2 large cloves of garlic crushed
$^1/_2$ tsp sugar
12 black olives
5 tomatoes cored, peeled and roughly chopped
salt and pepper
4 small red snapper gutted, scaled and well rinsed
50 ml dry white wine

Heat the oven to 200°C.

Heat the olive oil in a large frying pan until it is hot but not smoking. Add the onion, leeks, herbs, sugar and olives and gently fry them without browning for 5 minutes. Add the tomatoes and continue cooking until the mixture has reduced to a thick sauce. Season well with salt and pepper.

Take off the heat. Make 3 diagonal cuts in the topside of each fish. Spoon a little of the sauce inside each fish and arrange them side by side in a baking dish. Pour the remaining sauce around the fish and pour in the wine. Bake uncovered for 20 minutes until the fish flakes.

Enough for four.

WHOLE SNAPPER BAKED WITH POTATOES AND ONIONS

100 g butter
2 large onions sliced thinly
3 large cloves garlic crushed
3 tb parsley chopped
$1/2$ tsp sugar
1 whole snapper scaled and gutted, weighing
1.5–2 kg
3 large waxy potatoes sliced thinly and dried on
paper towels
$1^1/2$ tsp salt
freshly ground black pepper
100 ml dry white wine
150 ml water

Melt the butter over a gentle heat and fry the onions, garlic, parsley and sugar until the onions are soft and golden but not browned.

Put the fried onions into the bottom of a large casserole and put the whole fish on top. Pack the potatoes around and over the fish. Sprinkle over the salt and plenty of freshly ground black pepper. Pour over the wine and the water.

Cover the casserole tightly (tin foil will do if there is no lid) and bake at 200°C for 1 hour or until the potatoes are cooked.

Serve in the casserole.

Serves six.

TARAKIHI WITH SCALLOPS, PERNOD AND SORREL

75 g butter
4 fillets of tarakihi skinned and boned
flour for dusting fish
12 scallops sliced
300 g sorrel chopped
1 tb parsley chopped
25 ml Pernod
50 ml dry white wine
juice of half a lemon
salt
freshly ground black pepper

Melt the butter in a large frying pan over a gentle heat. Flour the fish and place in the butter. Fry gently for about 3 minutes on each side so that the fillets are golden brown and just cooked. Take the fish fillets out of the frying pan and put them onto a serving dish. Keep them warm in a hot oven.

Add the scallops, sorrel and parsley to the pan. Give the pan a few shakes so that the scallops are cooked in the butter and the sorrel begins to melt. Pour in the Pernod, let it bubble, then add the wine and lemon juice.

Let the mixture bubble until the scallops are just cooked and the liquid is syrupy. Pour in any juice that has seeped out of the fish onto the serving dish. Add a pinch of salt and a little black pepper. Pour the mixture over the fish and serve immediately.

Serves four.

JOHN DORY PAN-FRIED WITH MUSSELS

75 g butter
flour for dusting fish
4 skinned and boned fillets of John Dory weighing
about 150 g each
2 spring onions finely chopped
half a small carrot cut into 5mm dice
half a stick of celery cut into 5mm dice
1 tb parsley chopped
1 tb chives chopped
75 ml dry white wine or cider
16 mussels steamed open in 1 cup water, reserve
100 ml of the strained cooking liquid
salt and pepper

Heat the oven to 200°C.

Melt the butter in a large frying pan. Flour the fish and pan-fry for 2 minutes on each side. Add the spring onions, celery, carrot and herbs and give the pan a shake. Pour in the wine or cider and the mussel liquid. Put the pan in the hot oven for 8 minutes or until the fish is cooked. Take the fish out and put it on a serving dish and keep it hot.

Add the mussels to the pan and heat them over a gentle heat. Let the liquid reduce slightly. Taste and season with salt and pepper. Pour the mussel mixture over the fish and serve.

Serves four.

JOHN DORY OR SALMON FILLETS
EN PAPILLOTE

'En papillote' means baked in a paper case which is made from a circle of strong, greaseproof paper. The fish is put in the middle, then the paper is folded into a semi-circle, then the edges are folded together a dozen times so that it is sealed. It is a chef's technique and I have noticed few chefs have very much success with it, so my advice is to use tin foil — it works just as well. The advantage of cooking fish in this way is that the juices and aroma are sealed inside until you open your individual package. It works extremely well for barbecues.

4 fillets of John Dory or salmon, about 150 g each,
skinned and boned
200 g butter
1 carrot and 2 sticks of celery cut into
matchsticks
$1/2$ small onion or 2 shallots very finely chopped
1 tb fresh tarragon leaves
50 ml dry white wine
pepper and salt

Heat the oven to 200°C.

Cut 4 pieces of tin foil big enough to accommodate the fish fillets. Put a fillet on each one, ready for the vegetables.

Melt 150 g of butter in a large frying pan over a gentle heat. Fry the vegetables and tarragon very gently without browning until the the vegetables are tender. Add the wine and continue to cook the mixture until the liquid has almost evaporated. Taste the mixture and season well with salt and freshly ground black pepper. Divide the mixture into 4 portions and carefully place a portion on each fillet of fish.

Cut the remaining butter into 4 parts. Put a piece of butter on each portion. Pull up the sides of the tin foil and twist the edges together so that you have 4 sealed packages that are not tight against the fish. Put the packages on to an ovenproof baking dish and bake for 15 minutes, or place on a moderately hot barbecue.

Open the package at the table. The smell is delicious.

Serves four.

FRIED FISH IN A SPICE CRUST

**700 g firm white fish fillets cut into pieces about
4 cm x 10 cm.
flour for dusting
1 egg beaten with 1 cup milk**

**SPICE CRUST
300 g breadcrumbs
3 cloves garlic finely chopped
1 tb ground turmeric
3 tb ground cumin
1 tb ground black pepper
finely grated zest of 2 lemons
1/2 tsp cayenne pepper
Mix together well and set aside.**

Dust the pieces of fish with flour, dip them in the egg and milk, then in the spiced breadcrumbs, patting well so they stick.

Gently fry in hot oil until golden brown and cooked through.

Drain on paper towels and serve with chopped coriander and lemon wedges.

Serves four.

FISH STEAKS BRAISED WITH CHILLIS, BLACK BEANS AND DRIED MUSHROOMS

I ate a great fish dish in the Lac Canh Restaurant in Nha Trang, Vietnam. This is my approximation.

4 tb soy bean oil
4 red chillis split lengthways in half
2 hapuku or groper steaks, 500 g approx.
4 tb light soy sauce
4 tb fish sauce
500 ml fish stock
2 tb Chinese fermented black beans, well washed under cold water, and drained
1 tb sugar
8 spring onions, white part only
8 Chinese dried mushrooms, soaked in hot water for 30 minutes, drained, stems discarded, sliced
100 g glass noodles (also called bean thread or cellophane noodles) soaked 30 minutes in hot water, drained
fresh coriander

Heat oil in large frying pan until hot but not smoking. Add the chillis and stirfry 20 seconds. Add the fish and sear both sides. Add everything else, except the noodles and coriander. Simmer until the fish is just cooked. Taste and add more soy or fish sauce; if it is too salty add a little water.

Put the fish on a hot serving dish, with the vegetables around it.

Add the drained noodles to the cooking liquid and simmer 1 minute, until the noodles are transparent.

Put the noodles on top of the fish.

Pour over some of the cooking liquid and garnish with plenty of coriander, to be eaten as a green with the fish.

Serves four.

KUMARA STUFFING FOR WHOLE BAKED FISH

100 g butter
1 large golden kumara peeled and grated
1 tb ginger finely chopped
2 tb parsley chopped
1 onion finely chopped
1 clove garlic chopped
1 stick of celery sliced
125 g almonds roasted and roughly chopped
100 ml dry white wine
salt and pepper, lemon juice

A whole snapper or baby red snapper are delicious with this stuffing.

Melt the butter in a frying pan over a gentle heat. Add all the ingredients except the wine, fish and seasonings and stir well so that they become well coated with butter. Very gently fry the mixture, without browning it, for 8 minutes. Add the wine and simmer gently until all the liquid has disappeared. Season with the salt, pepper and lemon juice.

Put the fish in a large, oiled baking dish. Fill the cavity with the stuffing, sprinkle with a little white wine or water, dot the fish with butter and cover with tin foil. Bake in a very hot oven until the fish flakes or until a knife can be pulled out cleanly (about 10 minutes per 500 g).

POACHED FISH WITH SAUCE ROUILLE

**1.5 kg white fish fillets skinned and boned
(hapuku, tarakihi, gurnard, snapper, John Dory are
all suitable)
3 tomatoes peeled, cored and roughly chopped
1 onion sliced
1 sprig parsley
1 sprig fresh thyme
1 bay leaf
6 peppercorns
$^1/_2$ tsp salt
50 ml dry white wine
water
200 ml rouille (see page 35)
chopped parsley**

Heat the oven to 200°C.

Choose a large frying pan or ovenproof dish. Place the fish in the
pan or dish and put all the other ingredients except the rouille
around it. Pour in enough water just to cover the fish. Over a fast
heat, bring to the boil. Put the dish in the oven and poach for 15
minutes or until the fish flakes.

Carefully remove the fish from the poaching liquid and drain well.
Arrange the fish on a serving dish (use the herbs, vegetables and
liquid for a soup) and sprinkle with chopped parsley.

Serve with a bowl of rouille on the side.

Plenty for six.

Smoked Fish

SMOKED FISH SALAD

1 carrot peeled and sliced very thinly
half a telegraph cucumber sliced thinly
1 stick celery sliced thinly
1 tsp salt
250 g smoked fish, skinned, boned and flaked
1 tsp drained capers
1 small lettuce washed and torn into bite-sized
pieces
1 gherkin chopped roughly
1 cooked potato peeled and cut into 1 cm dice
1 tb parsley chopped
100 ml olive oil
juice of 1 lemon
2 tb red wine vinegar
pepper and salt

Put the carrot, cucumber and celery into a china bowl and sprinkle over 1 tsp salt. Mix the vegetables so that they are all covered with salt. This salt treatment will make them sweat and pickle them slightly. Set aside for 30 minutes, then rinse them well under cold water and squeeze them dry. Put all the ingredients into a salad bowl.

Make a vinaigrette by mixing together the olive oil, lemon juice and red wine vinegar. Season with pepper and salt and pour over the salad.

Turn the salad over a few times and serve with fresh bread.
Serves four.

AÏOLI GARNI (FOR GARLIC LOVERS)

Make 300 ml of aïoli (garlic mayonnaise, see page 21) and put it
into an attractive bowl in the middle of the biggest serving platter
you have.

Around it put some sliced smoked roes and plenty of boned, flaked
smoked fish. Put some well-washed crisp lettuce leaves around
the platter and on them pile carrots and celery cut into strips, artichoke hearts, black olives, wedges of tomato, well-washed radish-
es with their green tops left on, blanched broccoli and cauliflower,
some hardboiled eggs cut in half, a few capers and some spring
onions.

Serve with plenty of french bread and cool white wine as an hors
d'oeuvre or a summer lunch. Give your guests a plate each and
watch them attack.

Serves six.

SOFT ROES

These creamy delicacies can be treated like lambs' — or calves' — brains, though their flavour is quite different. Poach them for a few seconds in gently boiling water to make them firm and easy to handle or, if you are careful, use them as they are.

FRESH ROE WITH LEMON AND CAPERS

100 g butter
6-8 fresh roes rinsed under cold water
flour for dusting
1 lemon peeled and sliced around the core
(discard the core), flesh cut into 1 cm dice
2 tb capers
1 tb parsley chopped
25 ml white wine
pepper and salt

Heat the butter in a large frying pan until it bubbles but does not burn. Dust the roes in the flour and fry them in the butter until they are firm and golden. Remove them to a hot serving dish and keep them warm.

Add the lemon dice, capers, parsley and wine to the pan and boil for a few seconds or until the mixture is hot and syrupy. Season with salt and freshly ground black pepper.

Pour the mixture over the roes and serve with crusty bread and salad.

A tasty lunch for four.

SOFT ROE FRITTERS

6 fresh roes chopped
2 eggs
2 tb of flour
1 large boiled floury potato mashed
half a small onion very finely diced
1 tb parsley chopped
1 tb fresh coriander chopped
$1/2$ tsp salt
olive oil for frying

Mix all the ingredients except the oil to a thick purée. Do not use a food processor as this will make the mixture too fine and the flavour nondescript. Heat almost a centimetre of olive oil in a heavy frying pan until it is very hot. Drop spoonfuls of the mixture into the hot oil and cook them until they are crisp and golden. Drain them well and keep them warm until all the mixture is used.

Serve with lemon wedges and more chopped parsley.

Serves two.

Raw Fish

POISSON CRU

**600 g snapper or fine white fish fillets, skinned,
boned and sliced thinly
2 spring onions finely sliced
1 small clove garlic finely chopped
1 green capsicum cored, seeded and finely sliced
1 stick celery thinly sliced
1 cup snow pea sprouts, or better still, if you can
find them, fresh fenugreek sprigs
pepper and salt
1 tb ginger finely chopped
3 tb coriander leaves**

Mix everything well and refrigerate 15 minutes.

Serve as a first course with lime wedges to squeeze over it.

Serves four.

KOKODA WITH POPPADOMS

Kokoda is the celebrated Fijian marinated fish in coconut cream.

600 g firm white fish fillets, skinned, boned and cut into 2 cm cubes

Sprinkle well with vinegar and leave to marinate 2 hours. Rinse carefully with cold water and drain well.

$1/2$ cup fresh lime juice
1 hot green chilli seeded and chopped finely
200 ml coconut cream
1 tomato cored, seeded and cut into 2 cm dice
$1/2$ red capsicum cored, seeded and chopped
1 spring onion sliced
coriander leaves
pepper and salt

Pour lime juice and coconut cream over the fish and mix well. Set aside 20 minutes. Mix in the other ingredients. Taste and season with salt and pepper.
Serve with hot poppadoms.
Serves four.

CEVICHE (SOUTH AMERICAN RAW FISH MARINATED IN LEMON JUICE)

500 g boned, skinned snapper cut into 5 cm dice
150 ml lemon or lime juice or a mixture of both
1 large, boiled golden kumara peeled and cut into
3 cm dice
1 green chilli chopped finely
1 spring onion chopped finely
100 g whole kernel sweetcorn rinsed in cold water
3 large tomatoes cored, seeded and roughly
chopped
2 tb parsley chopped
1 tb fresh coriander chopped
$^1/_2$ tsp sugar
salt and pepper

Put the fish into an earthenware bowl and pour the lemon or lime juice over it. Let it marinate for 2 hours. Add all the other ingredients except the salt and pepper and marinate for another hour. Taste and season with salt and freshly ground black pepper. Serves four.

Flounder

FRIED MARINATED FLOUNDER

4-6 small fresh flounder, gutted
milk
seasoned flour
olive oil

MARINADE
4 tb olive oil
1 small onion finely sliced
1 large clove of garlic finely chopped
1 yellow or red capsicum grilled, skinned, cored
and seeded
4 tb dry white wine
4 tb wine vinegar
1 tsp sugar
salt and pepper

Dip the fish in the milk, drain it and dredge it in the flour.

Heat the oil in a large frying pan until it is hot but not smoking. Fry the fish in the hot oil until it is crisp and golden. Drain the fish and pack them closely into a deep serving dish.

THE MARINADE

Heat the oil in a saucepan and very gently fry the onion and garlic for about 5 minutes or until they are soft and golden.

Cut the capsicum into fine strips, add to the pan and fry for 1 minute. Stir in the wine, vinegar, sugar and a good pinch of salt and a little pepper. Bring to the boil and simmer for 1 minute. Pour the marinade over the fish. Cover and leave overnight to be eaten cold the next day.

Serves four.

FLOUNDER FILLETS IN ASIAN BROTH

4 cloves garlic chopped
1^1/$_2$ tb coriander root chopped
3 shallots chopped
2 stalks lemon grass, bulbous ends only, peeled
and chopped
^{1}/$_2$ tsp white peppercorns ground
zest of 1 lime
^{1}/$_2$ cup water

Purée to a smooth paste in a food processor.
Gently fry in 2 tb vegetable oil until the water has evaporated, the
paste is fragrant and the oil is seeping out of the mixture.

750 ml fish stock
2 cups water
12 fresh wonton wrappers, cut in half diagonally
6 dried Chinese mushrooms, soaked in hot water
for 20 minutes, stalks cut off, sliced
250 g flounder fillets, skinned, boned and
sprinkled with 2 tb fish sauce
3 spring onions sliced
^{1}/$_2$ cup coriander leaves

Bring stock to the boil. Add the fried paste, mushrooms and won-
ton wrappers.
Simmer 4 minutes until the wonton wrappers are tender.
Add the flounder, spring onions and coriander.
Bring to the boil and serve immediately.
Serves four.

MARINE FISH

FLOUNDER WITH PARMESAN

fresh flounder
butter
finely grated Parmesan
white wine
lemon juice
chopped parsley
lemon wedges

Fry the flounder in hot butter until crisp and golden on both sides. Before it is cooked through, sprinkle a thick layer of Parmesan on top of each fish. Sprinkle over a little white wine and a squeeze of lemon juice and put the frying pan into a hot oven.

The fish will finish cooking and the cheese, wine and butter will amalgamate into a thick sauce.

Serve with lemon wedges and sprinkle with chopped parsley.

A dish of hot fresh fettucine with plenty of garlic butter stirred through it completes the meal.

Tuna

Tuna needs to be handled differently from most fish. If you are lucky enough to catch fresh tuna, nothing is better than immediate sashimi (Japanese-style raw fish, thinly sliced, served with soy sauce and wasabi).

When grilling, barbecuing or frying tuna, it benefits from being cooked medium rare as it becomes dry and tasteless if completely cooked.

TUNA WITH LEMON AND MINT

This makes an excellent hors d'oeuvre

Take enough of the following for your purpose:
thinly sliced lemons
1/2 cm thick slices raw tuna skinned and boned
fresh mint leaves
salt and freshly ground black pepper
olive oil

Place a small slice of tuna on a lemon slice. Season with salt and pepper. Place a whole mint leaf on top. Drizzle with olive oil. Serve.

CURED TUNA WITH GINGER AND CORIANDER

700 g fresh tuna fillet (bluefin, yellowfin or bigeye), skinned, boned and cut lengthways into 2 cm thick slabs
$1^1/_2$ tb brown sugar
$1^1/_2$ tb Maldon sea salt
1 tb ginger cut into very thin matchsticks
1 tb coriander stalks finely chopped

Mix the salt and sugar and rub all over the tuna. Place in a non-reactive dish just big enough to hold it and sprinkle the ginger and coriander over the fish. Cover and refrigerate for 24 hours, turning twice.

Serve thinly sliced as an hors d'oeuvre with coriander sprigs, sliced avocado and tomatoes.

Serves four to six.

FRESH TUNA NIÇOISE
A loose interpretation of salad niçoise.

600 g fresh tuna, in 1 piece, skinned and boned
2 cloves garlic puréed with 1/2 cup olive oil and
1 tsp paprika

Rub the garlic oil all over the tuna and pan-fry until the tuna is medium rare, turning occasionally. Cool and slice 1 cm thick.

3 waxy potaoes, peeled, boiled, drained, cooled
and diced not too small
150 g green beans, dropped into boiling water for
2 minutes, refreshed under cold water, well
drained
2 cups cherry tomatoes halved
6 artichoke halves (tinned are fine, just drain well
and toss in a little olive oil)
6 large green olives
2 cups baby salad greens
extra virgin olive oil
lemon wedges
salt and pepper
1 1/2 cups basic mayonnaise (see page 20) mixed
with 1/2 cup each of parsley and chervil leaves,
2 tb capers and 2 cloves finely chopped garlic.
Taste and season with salt and pepper.
Set aside.

Put everything on a large platter in separate piles; put the mayonnaise in a small bowl. Drizzle the fish and vegetables with the extra virgin olive oil and garnish with lemon wedges.
Serves four to six.

Mullet

GREY MULLET BAKED WITH ONIONS AND BASIL

1 whole grey mullet weighing about 1–1.5 kg
gutted and rinsed well, inside and out, under
running water
4 tb olive oil
3 onions sliced
1 clove of garlic crushed
1 large handful fresh basil leaves torn into pieces
2 tb parsley chopped
$1/2$ tsp sugar
1 lemon cut into thin slices
100 ml dry white wine
salt and pepper

Heat the oven to 200°C.

Pat the fish dry with paper towels and set to one side. Heat the oil over moderate heat in a large frying pan and add the onions, garlic, basil, parsley and sugar. Gently fry the mixture without browning until the onions are golden. Pour the onion mixture into a large baking dish to make a bed of onions.

Put the fish on top of the onions and arrange the lemon slices over the fish. Pour over the wine. Sprinkle over a little salt and freshly ground black pepper. Put the lid on the dish or cover it tightly with tin foil and bake for 25-30 minutes or until the fish flakes.

Serve with bread and salad.

This dish makes a very inexpensive and tasty meal for four.

GREY MULLET BRAISED WITH VEGETABLES

2 x 500 g grey mullet, scaled, gutted and the gut
cavity well washed so that the black film which
covers the gut cavity is removed. Slash the fish
diagonally 2 or 3 times on each side and set
aside.
50 ml olive oil
1 onion sliced
1 carrot peeled and cut into 1 cm dice
1 stick celery finely sliced
2 courgettes sliced
2 cloves garlic finely chopped
1 tsp sugar
2 tb capers
1 x 400 g whole peeled Italian tomatoes in juice,
cored and mashed
100 ml dry vermouth

In a large deep frying pan, heat the oil over moderate heat.

Add everything except the fish, tomatoes and vermouth and stir-fry over low heat without browning until the vegetables are soft, about 10 minutes. Add the tomatoes and vermouth and bring to the boil, simmer 3 minutes. Remove from the heat.

Preheat the oven to 200°C.

Take a baking dish which will hold the fish and vegetable mixture snugly and pour in half the vegetable mixture. Lie the fish on top side by side. Pour the remaining vegetables over the fish and bake uncovered 25 minutes until the fish is cooked.

Serve in the baking dish or carefully remove to a platter. Serves four to six.

MARINE FISH

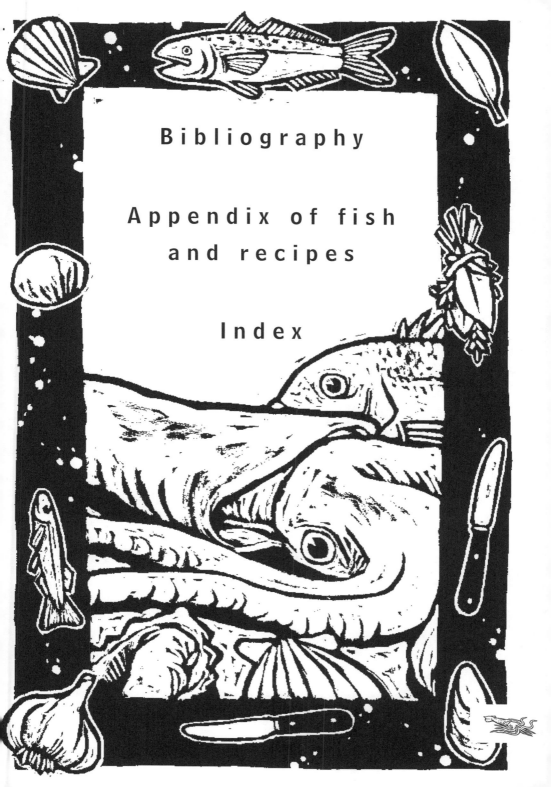

Bibliography

Appendix of fish
and recipes

Index

Bibliography

Armitage, Payne, Lockerly, Currie, Colban, Lamb & Phipps (eds),
   Guide Book to New Zealand Commercial Fish Species,
   NZ Fishing Industry Board, 1994.

David E., *French Country Cooking*, Penguin, 1970.

David E., *French Provincial Cooking*, Penguin, 1970.

David E., *Italian Cooking, Penguin,* 1981.

David E., *Mediterranean Cooking*, Penguin, 1972.

David E., *Summer Cooking*, Penguin, 1972.

Davidson A., *Mediterranean Seafood*, Penguin, 1976.

Forbes L., *Recipes from the Indian Spice Trail*, BBC Books, 1994.

Freeman M., *The Vietnamese Cookbook, Viking*, 1995.

Grigson J., *Fish Cookery*, Penguin, 1975.

Hazan M., *The Classic Italian Cookbook*, Macmillan, 1985.

Hazan M., *The Second Classic Italian Cookbook*, Macmillan, 1985.

Jaffrey M., *Far Eastern Cookery*, BBC Books, 1989.

Kalra J. Prasad, *Cooking with the Indian Masters*, Allied Publishers,
   1990.

Miles S., *A Taste of the Sea*, Heinemann, 1980.

Roden C., *A Book of Middle Eastern Food*, Penguin, 1982.

Tsuji S., *Japanese Cooking A Simple Art*, Kodansha International, 1980.

Willan A., *French Regional Cooking*, Hutchinson, 1981.

Appendix

WHAT TO MAKE WITH WHICH FISH
You have your fish, now what can you do with it? Many of the recipes can be used for other types of fish. The following list shows which recipes suit which fish. See also the chapter on sauces and accompaniments.

ALFONSINO
fillets: firm-textured fish with white flesh
scallops in broth with glass noodles
chilled coconut and seafood soup
seafood soup with spice paste
steamed seafood with soba noodles and greens
snapper with tofu and greens
fish broth with fettucine
New Zealand fish stew
bourride
Pierre's snapper with scallops and lovage
tarakihi with scallops and Pernod
fried fish fillets
fried fish in a spice crust
penne with olive oil and fish crumbs
fish steaks with chillis, black beans and dried mushrooms (use fillets instead of steaks)
John Dory pan-fried with mussels
South Indian fish and vegetable curry
kokoda with poppadoms
ceviche

ANCHOVY, PIPER (GARFISH), PILCHARD (SARDINE), SPRAT (NEW ZEALAND HERRING) AND YELLOW-EYED MULLET
whole, gutted darkish oily flesh with a distinct taste
fried, grilled or barbecued small fish
fried marinated flounder
sprats or yellow-eyed mullet with basil and garlic

BLUENOSE

fillets: firm, moist flesh which lightens on cooking

scallops in broth with glass noodles
steamed seafood with soba noodles and greens
chilled coconut and seafood soup
seafood soup with spice paste
snapper and tofu with greens and noodles
fish broth with fettucine
New Zealand fish stew
bourride
Pierre's snapper with scallops and lovage
salmon carpaccio with lime and ginger
tarakihi with scallops and Pernod
poisson cru
fried fish fillets
fish fried in a spice crust
penne with olive oil and fish crumbs
fish steaks with chillis, black beans and dried mushrooms (use fillets)
John Dory pan-fried with mussels
snapper with green herbs
South Indian fish and vegetable curry
poached fish with sauce rouille
John Dory or salmon en papillotte

BUTTERFISH (GREENBONE), GURNARD, JOHN DORY, MAOMAO, MOKI, SNAPPER, TARAKIHI, FILLETS AND WHOLE, HAPUKU

fillets and steaks: popular eating fish with white, juicy flesh suitable for most cooking methods.

scallops in broth with glass noodles
steamed seafood with soba noodles and greens
chilled coconut and seafood soup
snapper with tofu, greens and noodles
fish broth with fettucine
New Zealand fish stew
bourride
Pierre's snapper with scallops and lovage
salmon carpaccio with lime and ginger
tarakihi with scallops and Pernod
poisson cru

fried fish fillets

fried fish in a spice crust

fried marinated flounder (use fillets or hapuku steaks)

John Dory pan-fried with mussels

snapper with green herbs

kumara stuffing for whole baked fish (whole snapper and butterfish)

grey mullet baked with onions and basil (whole butterfish, gurnard,
small snapper, and hapuku steaks)

grey mullet braised with vegetables (whole butterfish gurnard, small
snapper and hapuku steaks)

baby red snapper baked with leeks and tomatoes (whole small butter
fish and gurnard)

flounder fillets in Asian broth

poached fish with sauce rouille

whole snapper baked with potatoes and onions (also John Dory with the
head removed, whole butterfish and gurnard, and hapuku steaks)

John Dory or salmon en papillotte

kokoda with poppadoms

ceviche

CARDINAL

fillets: moist, meaty flesh which lightens as cooked

scallops in broth with glass noodles

snapper with tofu, greens and noodles

New Zealand fish stew

fried fish in a spice crust

fried marinated flounder

penne with olive oil and fish crumbs

fish steaks with chillis, black beans and dried mushrooms (use fillets
and do not overcook)

South Indian fish and vegetable curry

grey mullet braised with vegetables (use fillets and do not overcook)

COD, BLUE

*fillets: white flesh suitable for most cooking methods. Sue Miles in her
excellent* Taste of the Sea *(Heinemann 1980) recommends salting the fillets well before use, putting them in the refrigerator for 2 hours, wiping
dry then cooking.*

scallops in broth with glass noodles

steamed seafood with soba noodles and greens

chilled coconut and seafood soup

snapper with tofu, greens and noodles
fish broth with fettucine
tarakihi with scallops and Pernod
fried fish fillets
John Dory pan-fried with mussels
flounder fillets in Asian broth

COD, RED
fillets: delicate white, moist flesh, do not overcook
steamed seafood with soba noodles and greens
snapper with tofu, greens and noodles
Pierre's snapper with scallops and lovage
tarakihi with scallops and Pernod
fried fish in a spice crust
grey mullet braised with vegetables (use fillets and do not overcook)
flounder fillets in Asian broth

CREAMFISH
see also Leatherjacket, Flounder recipes and Sole, whole, gutted and fillets: sweet delicate white flesh, very good eating
steamed seafood with soba noodles and greens (fillets)
chilled coconut and seafood soup (fillets)
fish broth with fettucine (fillets)
poisson cru (fillets, skinned)
fried fish fillets
flounder fillets in Asian broth

GARFISH, SEE ANCHOVY

GREENBONE, SEE BUTTERFISH

GURNARD, SEE BUTTERFISH

HAPUKU, SEE BUTTERFISH

HERRING NEW ZEALAND, SEE ANCHOVY

JOHN DORY, SEE BUTTERFISH

KAHAWAI

fillets: dark flesh, can take strong flavours, bleed well before filleting
New Zealand fish stew
fish steaks with chillis, black beans and dried mushrooms (use fillets)
fried marinated flounder (use fillets)
grey mullet baked with onions and basil
grey mullet braised with vegetables
baby red snapper baked with leeks and tomatoes

KINGFISH

fillets or steaks: darkish flesh which lightens when cooked, treat like tuna, makes great sashimi
chilled coconut and seafood soup
New Zealand fish stew
salmon carpaccio with lime and ginger
salmon in sweet soy
poisson cru
fried marinated flounder (use fillets)
grey mullet baked with onions and basil
grey mullet braised with vegetables
ceviche

LEATHERJACKET(CREAMFISH)

use gutted, skinned and head removed: very white sweet flesh, often quite thick so they need careful cooking
New Zealand fish stew
fried fish fillets (use whole, head removed and skinned)
fried or barbecued small fish
fried marinated flounder
fish steaks with chillis, black beans and dried mushrooms
South Indian fish and vegetable curry
grey mullet baked with onions and basil
grey mullet braised with vegetables
baby red snapper baked with leeks and tomatoes
whole snapper baked with potatoes and onions

LEMONFISH

fillets: very firm white flesh, can take strong flavours and does not fall apart in stews or when baked, but do not overcook
New Zealand fish stew

bourride
fried fish fillets
fried fish in a spice crust
fish steaks with chillis, black beans and dried mushrooms
John Dory pan-fried with mussels
South Indian fish and vegetable curry
grey mullet braised with vegetables (use fillets)
baby red snapper baked with leeks and tomatoes (use fillets)
kokoda with poppadoms
ceviche

LING
fillets: white flesh, firm texture, does not fall apart when cooked
scallops in broth with glass noodles
New Zealand fish stew
South Indian fish and vegetable curry
grey mullet baked with onions and basil (use fillets)
grey mullet braised with vegetables (use fillets)
baby red snapper baked with leeks and tomatoes (use fillets)

MACKEREL
small whole gutted or fillets: dark oily flesh, can take strong flavours
fried marinated flounder (small whole fish)
fried grilled or barbecued small fish

MAOMAO, SEE BUTTERFISH

MOKI, SEE BUTTERFISH

MONKFISH AND ORANGE ROUGHY
fillets: white, firm flesh with a prawn or crayfish-like texture and delicate taste
scallops in broth with glass noodles
steamed seafood with soba noodles and greens
chilled coconut and seafood soup
snapper with tofu, greens and noodles
New Zealand fish stew
bourride
Pierre's snapper with scallops and lovage
fried fish in a spice crust

penne with olive oil and fish crumbs
John Dory pan-fried with mussels
South Indian fish and vegetable curry
ceviche

MULLET, GREY

whole, gutted and cavity well washed: sweet, slightly oily, firm flesh, bakes, grills and barbecues well
grey mullet baked with onions and basil
grey mullet braised with vegetables
baby red snapper baked with leeks and tomatoes
yellow-eyed mullet with basil and garlic

ORANGE ROUGHY, SEE MONKFISH

PILCHARD, SEE ANCHOVY

PIPER, SEE ANCHOVY

SALMON, TROUT AND SALMON TROUT, SEE CHAPTER ON FRESHWATER FISH

SARDINE, SEE ANCHOVY

SNAPPER, SEE BUTTERFISH

SOLE, SEE FLOUNDER RECIPES

SPRAT, SEE ANCHOVY

TARAKIHI, SEE BUTTERFISH

TREVALLY

fillets: rich flavour with darkish flesh which lightens on cooking, good eating
scallops in broth with glass noodles

steamed seafood with soba noodles and greens
chilled coconut and seafood soup
snapper with tofu, greens and noodles
fish broth with fettucine
New Zealand fish stew
salmon in sweet soy
tarakihi with scallops and Pernod
fried fish fillets
fish steaks with chillis, black beans and dried mushrooms (use fillets)
John Dory pan-fried with mussels
South Indian fish and vegetable curry
John Dory or salmon en papillotte
ceviche

TUNA, SEE TUNA RECIPES

WAREHOU, SILVER, BLUE
fillets: pinkish flesh which lightens when cooked, versatile, can be fried,
grilled or baked
scallops in broth with glass noodles
steamed seafood with soba noodles and greens
seafood soup with spice paste
New Zealand fish stew
salmon carpaccio with lime and ginger
poisson cru
fried fish fillets
fried fish in a spice crust
fried marinated flounder
penne with olive oil and fish crumbs
John Dory pan-fried with mussels
South Indian fish and vegetable curry
grey mullet braised with vegetables (use fillets)
baby red snapper baked with leeks and tomatoes
poached fish with sauce rouille
kokoda with poppdoms
ceviche

YELLOW-EYED MULLET, SEE ANCHOVY

Index

INDEX

INDEX

Ray McVinnie describes himself as a food enthusiast, one of the few chefs he knows who has always cooked at home outside working hours. He feels this speaks volumes about his commitment to food.

Born and raised in the Waikato, he completed a masters degree in history at Auckland University.

He learnt to cook while working in restaurants as a student and by watching the chefs he was lucky enough to work with. In 1978 he opened Orleans Restaurant. After selling Orleans he continued as a professional chef, working at such well-known restaurants as The French Cafe, Raffles, Vinnies and for six years at Metropole. An experienced caterer, consultant and food stylist, he has judged the New Zealand Cheese Awards, the Corbans Wine and Food Challenge and is an assessor for the Beef and Lamb Hallmark of Excellence. He has travelled extensively in Asia researching food and worked there presenting New Zealand food to the Asian hospitality industry and the Asian public. He is a regular contributor to Cuisine magazine and teaches at the Epicurean Workshop in Auckland. He has retired from being a full-time chef to pursue his other food interests.

He lives in Auckland with his partner and their two children.